HEAVEN
BECKONS

Discover the Glory That Awaits You in the Afterlife

HEAVEN
BECKONS

B.W. MELVIN

DESTINY IMAGE® PUBLISHERS, INC.
P.O. Box 310, Shippensburg, PA 17257-0310
"Publishing cutting-edge prophetic resources to supernaturally empower the body of Christ"

This book and all other Destiny Image and Destiny Image Fiction books are available at Christian bookstores and distributors worldwide.

For more information on foreign distributors, call 717-532-3040.
Reach us on the Internet: www.destinyimage.com.

ISBN 13 TP: 978-0-7684-7717-7
ISBN 13 eBook: 978-0-7684-7718-4
ISBN 13 Hardcover: 978-0-7684-8129-7
ISBN 13 Large Print: 978-0-7684-8130-3

For Worldwide Distribution, Printed in the U.S.A.
1 2 3 4 5 6 7 8 / 28 27 26 25 24

ACKNOWLEDGMENTS

For all those who take time to look up the scripture references in this book, may you shine bright for Jesus in the midst of this dark world.

CONTENTS

PROLOGUE

WHERE ANGELS DANCE

"To an inheritance incorruptible and undefiled and that does not fade away, reserved in heaven for you."
—1 Peter 1:4 NKJV

There were about 19 of us from Campus Christian Ministries inside the hospital chapel. I knew that what I had to do was not in line with the others in the room.

"Sister Margaret's mother has late-stage cancer. She is in the hospital, hospice care, right now. We know God will heal her," Chaplain Barry of Campus Ministries said.

I could hear the group agreeing in unison, praying, "Betty will be healed…by His stripes she will be healed. We declare she will live and not die as a testimony for Jesus Christ. We believe and doubt not, oh Lord, for we know Thou art our healer. This disease is not unto death. We believe and shall receive…"

Early that morning, I woke up with a great burden to pray for Betty. So much so that I got on my knees and prayed about what to do. In the stillness, I heard the Lord speak to me in a quiet voice, saying simply, "Tell her of heaven."

"What, Lord? Is this really You, Jesus?"

"She has a fear of leaving her family behind."

That was it. Nothing else was said. I knew I had to speak to Betty about heaven.

* * *

The campus ministry, all 19, had gathered in Betty's hospital room. How could I interrupt and not sound unkind? As I leaned back quietly in the only chair in the room, all were praying and telling her that she would be healed. *Did I hear wrong?* As the scene unfolded, I heard positive, nice words, decrees, and declarations of healing. "We know You love Betty, Lord. We command the cancer to be rescinded." I sat there quietly, not able to shake off what I had been told.

Suddenly, the door opened and the most beautiful nurse I had ever seen entered the room. A radiance of white light gently emitted from her skin. With authority she directed kindly but firmly, "Alright, Betty needs to rest now, everyone out now. Thank you all for coming and praying. She needs rest, so you all will need to leave…"

Glancing at me with eyes of great depth and authority, she literally pointed to me and said directly, "You, stay, the rest must go now—out! Thank you for coming, hospital policy…"

The group left the room without paying attention to me. The nurse, in yellow scrubs, stood in the doorway and continued to thank the group for coming. Their joyful banter and footsteps faded down the hall. She turned toward me, smiled, and for a split second I thought she had wings of light, which disappeared as she shut the door.

I got up and approached the bed, "Hi Betty!"

Betty replied, "Oh, I thank you all for coming and praying, and that was so very nice…"

I plunged in. "Betty, this may be a strange question, but what do you really want prayer for right now?"

"Why is that strange? You all came and prayed such nice prayers…"

"Well, strange because I heard the Lord speak to me today, to tell you something…"

She smiled big. "Tell me. What did He have to say?"

"Betty, He told me to ask you a question, and the question is, what do you really want prayer for—I mean really?"

Betty met my eyes. "Will you pray for my family? I'm afraid their faith will fail, shipwrecked because of me. I can't leave till I know. I have seen angels dance, seen the Lord on high smiling—oh, His smile! You've seen Him too, haven't you? I'm not afraid for me—I fear for my family."

Christian people under hospice care often speak about seeing angels dance and heaven beckoning them. They also say things no one else knows about.

"Betty, I am one of those who died, and the Lord, by His grace alone, allowed me to come back and later showed me heaven. Does this sound strange? If it does, I can leave now."

"Oh, no, please stay. Your eyes are different. You are not like the others."

"Let's pray for your family as you asked; is that okay now?"

"Yes,"

"Heavenly Father, I ask that Betty's family *will* endure her departure. They believe she will be healed, but do not understand the true healing that awaits. I ask that they be strengthened and not fall away from You, Lord Jesus. Lord, we put every member of her family in Your hands." As we continued, Betty prayed and lifted each member of her family to the Lord.

I can't recall all I prayed or said that evening, but at the final amen Betty looked up as we held each other's hands and thanked me. "I feel peace now; anything else the good Lord wanted to share (*cough*) with me?"

"He wanted me to tell you about heaven and not to be afraid to leave. He has it all under control. So let me share what it is like to depart. Would you like that?"

"Yes, just don't want my family…shipwreck…faith (*cough*)."

I prayed again for her family's faith not to be shipwrecked by her departure and continued. "Okay, how do you feel now?"

"Better, thank you. You are the only one to ask me what I really wanted prayer for (*cough*), thank you."

"Let me share with you about departing."

"Yes…ready (*cough*)."

"He's calling you, isn't He?"

"Yes, He is…all the angels…"

I nodded, "I can't see them, but I feel the presence of heaven here."

"Oh, I want to go, but my family…"

I recall looking into her eyes, so worried about her family. She loved them so much. At the time, I did not know her family was steeped in faulty doctrine about healing, signs, wonders, and miracles.

She was afraid that if she passed on, their faith in Jesus would somehow be destroyed. I was struck by the thought that her chief concern was for her family's love and commitment to Jesus. She was afraid her passing would cause them to lose their love for the Lord.

With that I said, "Yes, I understand why you are afraid to leave. But let me share what it is like to pass on to where heaven beckons and the angels dance.

"Departing will seem strange at first. You will arise out of your body. You will see your earthly body for a moment, and you will become more alive than you are now. You will feel great peace. All pain disappears.

"Whatever you do, do not jump back, just ride on up. Everything will be explained to you. You will arrive at what the Bible describes as a sheep gate and Jesus will welcome you."

Betty replied, "Yes, I've seen that so far above me. Go on (*cough*). I've no one to tell this to. I know He is beckoning me to come, but I keep jumping back. My family…my family…"

We smiled at each other. "I understand Betty," I said. "The Lord hears your heart."

Betty feebly pointed upward, "Tell me more. It is so glorious. Can't you see? The wall is open, angels sing—a pathway!"

"Yes, that beautiful pathway leads to a gate, a great whitish, living, blue swirling pearly gate of heaven."

"Oh, I have seen that, where the angels dance…from a distance." Betty spoke as she squeezed my hand, "I want to go so bad, this pain, this body. My family (*cough*)."

"Yes, the angels go forth to do things for the Lord. You will enter through the great pearly gate and arrive at a grand meadow and enter that land of liquid love. Don't be afraid when you leave your body. It is okay to leave. Jesus has your family. He is faithful, understand?"

"Yes."

"Betty, let's pray. Lord Jesus, Betty is ready to depart to her homecoming and reward. Let it be, with great peace and real soon. She has seen Your angels sing and dance. Grant her great peace that her family is secure in Your hands. I ask that Betty depart in peace, in Jesus' name, amen."

Betty looked at me with glassy eyes and smiled big. "I am ready...so tired...great peace...great peace (*cough*)."

I smiled back, "I am leaving now so you can rest. We will meet in that field of reunion, that grand meadow someday, Betty."

"God bless you (*cough*)...bless you." She squeezed my hand and smiled.

I smiled in return, slowly leaving the room and quietly shutting the door. Then I went to the nurse's station to inquire about the nurse who wore yellow scrubs. I simply wanted to thank her. They said there was no one there on this floor wearing yellow scrubs. "No one wears those here, only green and blue. Strange!"

The next evening, I went to church where our campus ministry met. Everyone was extremely sad and let down. The chaplain had told them all that Betty passed away with the biggest, most pleasant smile he had ever seen.

The group bemoaned how they prayed and confessed her healing and all the prophecy received about her healing. *What happened? Who doubted? We prayed in faith believing we would receive. What happened?* Many in the group felt betrayed that Betty had not been healed, as they thought that would be best testimony for Jesus. I sat in silence and dared not speak. The chaplain had his own doubts to come to terms with.

He simply said something to the effect of, "Let's help Margret and her family. Who can cook meals? Let's realize in heaven is where one is finally healed of all things. Let us be the hands, feet, body of Christ, now, for Margret and her family."

Folks, this actually happened!

Some claim they know what is best for Jesus to do, and when it doesn't happen the way they want, shipwreck often follows. It is best to seek God and trust Him to know how to become

His hands, feet, and His body on earth as He directs, not as we imagine.

Equally tragic is how many in today's Western churches talk about a supernatural God, while at the same time saying God cannot do any supernatural things, like allowing someone to see heaven. For me, whether it was an open vision or taken there or not, you decide.

What I learned most from it is expressed within this simple, heartfelt prayer:

> *Lord Jesus,*
> *I deserved wrath, not mercy*
> *But I found grace instead*
> *You saved me*
> *I owe You my life*

I ask, can you make this your prayer?
Heaven beckons.

CHAPTER ONE

A PLACE CALLED HELL

"Who can say, 'I have made my heart pure; I am clean from my sin'?"

—Proverbs 20:9 ESV

December 1979 was my last Christmas before I died. Never did I think for a moment that roughly six months later I would find myself in hell. The inferno of that abyss haunted me. I am still processing what happened to this day.

I wrote about much of what happened in my first book, *A Land Unknown: Hell's Dominion*; although there was so much left out of it, with many things way too difficult to explain. Most amazing to me was that I was even allowed to return back to the land of the living. For that I owe Jesus Christ my very life. How about you? Can you say that?

I recall plainly the sights, sounds, smells, and even the terrible taste of that place. Also, experiencing what I named "eternal time" affects me to this day. How can you explain a place where time is no more, but rather eternal time without a linear feel to it—just continuing as past, present, and future?

The lost souls I saw in the abyss were alone, trapped in chambers of death (Proverbs 7:27), housed within cells just like in a dungeon (Isaiah 24:22), all within what the Bible calls the pit, a bottomless pit (Ezekiel 32:18-32). Reaping what they have sown. The real them exposed. This leaves a lasting impression on you. You learn what pride really means.

Hell uncovers the real you. Standing before Holy God and being judged right after you die is far more terrifying than witnessing hell. I went through that. Why I was even allowed to come back still puzzles me.

If God so wills to raise someone out of this place, why do so many spurn His sovereign will by declaring that He cannot? Pride is pride, no matter how one masquerades it.

Maybe I was permitted to come back simply to testify of the wonderous grace of our Lord and Savior, Jesus Christ. Maybe it was to leave a testimony against a world of near-death experiences (NDEs) that share that all will be well after you die. How so?

Competing voices speak of how many died, came back to life, and then tell everyone to head to the light. That there is no hell. All is heaven. No need for Jesus. It is all wonderful on the other side.

Well, if it sounds too good to be true, then it is. Yet folks pay no heed to that old maxim when it comes to such pleasant NDEs. They'll agree to this when it comes to the slick used car salesman, but not NDEs.

I saw people alone in cube-like cells surrounded by creatures emitting illusions of people and appearing as major props within these chambers of death. Each soul soon found themselves living in their own personal nightmare, never able to wake up. Just as one night terror ended another one began, over and over again.

I can't explain why being inside each small cell seemed to be as big as all outdoors or as small as an ant hole. Nor can I adequately explain what it was like walking in this awful place. It was like a hellish tour.

I was taken to a cell made just for me, that I knew full well I deserved. I was slowly dragged toward it. Then, when all hope vanished, He rescued me. After all these years, that alone affects me in a way that few will ever understand.

I saw so many folks within those cube-like cells. Each appeared to be living out scenes according to their time on earth in décor and areas they once lived. Each cell was small, but to those inside it appeared large.

I cannot fully explain the dimensions within the realm of eternal time. However, the deception that caused folks to come here very few can really grasp.

It is the nature of the demonic to be deceptive. They will go to any lengths, especially in their home turf, to trick people.

A person may at first see loved ones, butterflies, nice things, as well as feel love after arriving there. If resuscitated back to life, what do they report?

No need for Jesus. All make it to heaven. So many testimonies end up extoling new ageism, eastern mysticism, and/or gnostic thought.

Others who arrived in hell immediately entered their own personal torments. God was not torturing anyone there. They do it to themselves with the added help of the creatures there who remind them of that fact.

I saw so many folks arriving there thinking they were in paradise. Some stood before their beloved deities feeling bliss. Others felt great love by being welcomed by those who appeared as departed loved ones. A bit later, their nightmares began.

Medical science can, under the right conditions, bring one back to life. Most NDEs attest to this fact. Sometimes I feel like the person no one wants to hear on these matters, because my testimony shouts out loud: *If it sounds too good to be true then it is.*

Dying and coming back to life is a life-altering event. It overwhelms the senses. The devil takes advantage of such things to keep people away from the one sent to rescue them, Jesus reaches out to every living soul in many diverse ways, yet many fail to recognize His reach. Why?

The answers vary. Many NDEs report meeting departed loved ones. After that all is bliss because God is all love. Therefore, eternal recompense cannot exist. Don't worry!

Whatever the reason, the underlining thought brought back to this realm is that universalism's new age mindset is superior simply because such NDEs absolve everyone from consequences.

The hallmark of deception is to make God out as the oppressor and the new age god as the liberator for the oppressed. Look at all the NDEs that say there is no hell. Instead it's, "Do yoga. Love is love," or, worse yet, Christians are oppressors.

As an after-death survivor, I can't find fault with such NDE reports because continuing to exist after you die is an overwhelming experience. I get that better than most.

For example, despite being judged as guilty before the Lord and knowing I was heading to a horrible place, the first scene that greeted me was one of paradise, before it turned into hell. Such is deception. It tricks the mind. Many NDEs reflect this.

After I was allowed to return to this mortal realm, I was driven to the Bible. I cannot explain why. I died as an atheist, after all, but now no more.

What I discovered is that the word of God contained in the Bible teaches us how to be deceived no more. No longer controlled by the principality of the air. Able to reason and think as free men or women. The true oppressor is revealed along with his human minions and all their schemes.

That is why totalitarians hate this book that sets you free from deception. It exposes all tyrants' lies designed to turn folks away from God and unto themselves as one's only source of support.

Rain spattered against the windshield. Wiper blades rocked back and forth, interrupting my thoughts. Turning off the interstate, I managed to get all green lights. The radio station drew closer.

Pulling into the station's parking lot, I felt blessed to be allowed a glimpse of heaven because it helped me process why I saw a place called hell. How did it all begin?

CHAPTER TWO

THE RADIO SHOW

"Now you are the body of Christ, and members individually."
—1 Corinthians 12:27 NKJV

"This is ZWTW Christian Radio. Walk the walk and talk the talk, today."

Yes, being a guest on a popular radio show doesn't come easy with a testimony like mine. God opens and shuts doors.

"Tina, we have author-speaker B.W. Melvin back with us today!"

"That's right, Night Ryder. Last time he was with us we had so many phone calls. Glad to have you back!"

So goes the opening dialogue when you are being introduced. The earphones and microphone of the headset resting tightly upon my head reminded me that I was fortunate to be there. Why?

Back during the summer of 1980, I had one of those near-death—or, better said, after-death—experiences that folks like to talk so much about. By God's grace alone, I am still alive. You see, Jesus spared me from a very awful place. I owe Jesus Christ my life.

A few years after my death, I came face to face with Jesus in heaven, and to this day, almost 30 years later, I still remember His eyes. They change you.

My attention was turned to Night Ryder's voice booming from the headset, "Bryan, last time you were here, your experience sure shook up a whole lot of folks!"

"That's right," Tina Largo Crawford chimed in. "The phones really lit up, and for me, I can still smell the brimstone!"

"Well Tina, we'll be seeing a more pleasant side today…"

I sat there, cup of coffee in hand. All I could think of was hiking in the Rocky Mountains. So many things on earth are mere shadows compared to heaven's absolute grandeur. Looking back, I wondered what it was—perhaps a dream or an open vision, or what?

My mind began to drift through the traffic report, news, and weather while waiting for my cue. Memories of heaven swirled around. I imagined heaven—the walls and a pathway leading to the pearly gate chiseled by nails. There was a grand "field of reunion" free from tears or sorrows, and everything was new. And then there was the brilliant light of God. The atmosphere was pure liquid love. There were flowers, plants, and trees that quivered joyful praises to God. I saw a grand forest, great rural lands, and the great city, the New Jerusalem, being prepared.

I kept quiet about heaven for many years, only sharing it during brief occasions. Why was that?

For starters, my "heaven" experience was very personal. The purpose of my encounter in heaven was to heal me from experiencing that dreadful and terrifying place, the pit of hell. Another purpose was to assuage my fear of being classed as one of those wild-eyed, look-at-me, self-glory types, those uttering what is not lawful between heaven and hell—that which is mentioned in 2 Corinthians 12:4. Yes, it is true, some understandings about heaven are not lawful to utter.

Paul was not to utter all the things he saw because it would be done out of pride to promote himself. It would shift his eyes from God to himself. The root of pride has many branches. Self-promotion is very dangerous. (You are right to refer to the passage where the devil tempts Jesus to jump.) At this point, Paul should be thankful for his thorn in the flesh. We are not to glorify ourselves, but we are to bring glory to God.

I can testify to that. One of several reasons is that you learn characteristics of God's unfathomable nature that, if revealed, would cause some glory seeker to try to market these on earth.

Knowing such things would cause some folks to try to manipulate God's heart strings to get whatever they wanted on earth. Maybe the entity described in Ezekiel 28:11-19 did so; it mentions that "by the abundance of his trading he corrupted many."

Both Tina and Night Ryder ended the station break and picked up the conversation. "Bryan, before this interview we were discussing something you learned from your heaven experience that's intriguing concerning how the devil peddled secrets of heaven to humanity."

This is the way it goes in interviews; conversations go off in many directions. So, I responded, "I'll do my best to try to answer, if possible. We can go into more detail later on as I don't want to lose the audience. So I'll be brief. First off, like I asked before the show, is God true to His nature and character?"

"Yes, He cannot deny Himself in any manner. He is righteous in all His ways. He will never pervert justice," Ryder answered (Job 34:12).

Tina chimed in, "He is a God of truth. There is no injustice in Him. He is upright in all He does" (Deuteronomy 31:4).

"Yes," I said and added, "He is all powerfully able to work through all things beyond what our human minds can conceive. He is just and shows no partiality. He gave intelligent beings, whom He created to help and serve Him, a free moral will. If not, then how could God remain just?"

"I get that," Ryder stated. "I can see that with free will comes responsibility to live right before God and each other. With such responsibility, God tests and tries the reins of the heart. He fears nothing. He knows all things before anything ever was. So He knows beforehand how everyone will treat such responsibility."

Tina Largo entered the conversation, "Like we talked about before the show, God certainly foreknew that the one we call the devil would rebel. As I see it, it is almost like God is dividing darkness from light, teaching the difference between these two concepts. Letting folks like us and even the angels know what life is like without God versus life with Him. Does this make sense, Bryan?"

"Yes, that makes sense to me," I replied. "I learned things like this from heaven. It is not a new revelation or anything like that. It is deep, and I do not want to lose the folks listening."

Tina: "It's deep and fascinating. Makes you think. Bryan, please continue, I am sure our listeners would like to hear what you have to say."

"Okay, again I will try to be brief. Where to begin? For starters, let's look at how iniquity fosters rebellion and how it came about. Iniquity was found in the devil's heart as Ezekiel 28:15 points out. It was not placed there by God. The devil's hubris came by his own ability to freely reason that he could somehow exalt his throne above God's throne, as Isaiah 14:13 mentions."

"Before the interview, Bryan, you shared how this darkness come about?"

"Yes, first off as Ezekiel 28:14 states, he was one of the covering cherubim. He understood that God, in the absolute sense, is just to those whom He created to serve and help Him maintain creation. He knew due to God's life-giving nature that He will not extinguish anyone into a non-existent state of being."

"I have to ask, Bryan: why?"

"Short answer is this—doing so would cause God to deny who He is as God of the living (Ecclesiastes 3:11,14; 2 Samuel 14:14). The devil temporally got away with rebellion in a vain attempt to prove to God Himself that He cannot live up to His own standards of justice, righteousness, love.

"That old serpent understands God's nature is absolute. That God will never renege on any gift, calling, promise, or word spoken (Romans 11:29). Thus, he wrongly reasons that he can pit God's character traits and nature against each other in such way that would cause God to deny Himself, thus proving to the Lord God Himself that He is not true in all His ways.

"This will not happen. God cannot be outsmarted. He remains true to all that He is and, in the process, removes evil by first exposing what it is in a manner that's way beyond what our human minds can fully comprehend. We are living in that very timeframe, right now.

"This way, one can learn what life is like without God versus what life is like with Him—by living in an environment that exposes how good, kind, providing, gracious, and merciful God is versus how dominating and vile the way of darkness is.

"It is insane to try to tempt God to go against His own character and nature. Yet this world is under the sway of the evil one, causing people to unknowingly do the same today."

Night Ryder injected, "I see in Luke 4:1-13 the devil was trying the impossible—to entrap God Himself to go against His own words! Amazing!"

I replied. "Jesus certainly outsmarted the old serpent. He will never win."

"Amen!" Tina said in agreement.

"Tina and Ryder, can you image, if the deeper things about God's nature were made public, what some human agent would do with that kind of revelation?"

"I can see that Bryan, I can."

"Well, folks, time for another short station break. We'll be back in a moment with our guest who has a lot to say about heaven."

That is how interviews often go. You start out with a topic and the host goes in an unexpected direction. However, they know what they are doing—preparing the audience for what is to come in many clever ways.

As the next round of commercials, announcements, and weather reports droned on, I needed to refocus. My mind wandered back to heaven.

* * *

How can I ever explain heaven after all these years?

Magnificent living creatures reside there—angelic beings with wings of light, others riding on a disk of light just as the prophet Ezekiel described long ago. In heaven all people look about 30 years old, in the prime of life. They are without flaws, defects, or diseases. All are busy tending to the precious concerns of the Lord.

Oh, the little children there, millions of them—amazing!

Glorious sights are seen and music beyond mortal comprehension is heard. In heaven there exists no sorrow, no sadness,

no sickness, no death or tears. The river of life with its outflow-
ing tributaries meanders throughout heaven's land. In heaven,
the brilliance of God supplies the light and reveals His sovereign
glory and profound love. How could anyone ignore Him or
accuse His motives and intentions to be anything less than good
and perfect? In heaven, perfect gemstones reflect rainbows of
light declaring forth wondrous aspects of God's glorious nature
and character. Every shimmering stone reveals various aspects of
God's glory beyond description. Then there are the things that
no human words can describe as well as the things that cannot
be uttered.

Christian people really can't grasp what His glory means.
They pray for it to fall but have no idea of the weight, holiness,
cleansing, conviction that such glory brings.

When His glory fills the place, there is weight. It is notice-
able and tangible, often causing people to fall to the ground,
bow down, even weep, or listen in silence. During these times
of glory, great conviction often falls, and folks turn to Christ.
Other times, refreshing insights come. But the weightiness and
greatness of His glory relays a need for responsibility.

When we love God and care for and love one another,
God's glory is manifested on the earth. When we overlook these
responsibilities and put ourselves and our carnality first, we
completely miss the mark. God's glory is lost to us.

Yes, some things about heaven are not lawful to utter. This
fuels people to assume that no one can speak of or describe
heaven at all; thus, they accuse everyone with an afterlife experience as some sort of nutjob glory hound exploiting people for
money. Sadly, some do—but not all.

Despite the fakes, for purposes only known to the Lord,
He allows some folks to view a glimpse of heaven's eternity
and return to speak about it. After all, He is the God of truth,

revealing heaven's existence without divulging any secret things. He can do that, after all. He is God.

How can you tell the difference between the real and the fake?

First, true testimonies do not add to the Bible or replace scripture. The fakes are all about adding dramatic accounts in order to draw others to their made-up importance, whereas true testimonies increase faith in Jesus. What folks like me and others who have seen heaven have in common is that we do not seek glory for ourselves. We certainly are not special. For those who have had such an experience, we are humbled by it and often maligned for speaking about heaven, but not deterred from doing so.

We know there are things not lawful to utter and we will not do so. We speak of the things about heaven the Lord wants revealed, with permission. Thus, I mention only what He permits me to. Let's be cautious and not discount all such experiences due to the peddlers and glory hounds. Experiencing heaven and returning does happen. I suggest that you test all things. If these experiences point to Jesus alone and remain faithful to the gospel and to what is written in the Bible—pay attention. If not, yawn and go home.

Seeing heaven changes you in a good way. Seeing a false heaven does not. When that happens, self-glory grows. You can tell the difference.

Isaiah saw the throne room and was humbled by it (see Isaiah 6:1-4). He saw how his raw human condition was inadequate and needed cleansing. He received a coal of fire so as not to misuse God's words that God willed for him to utter later on. Seeing heaven likewise "undoes" you.

I myself received no new revelation or mandate. Seeing heaven simply healed my heart and began my journey of discovering how real the faithfulness of God is.

May the faithfulness of the Lord of Glory grant to you an infectious faith. Like Isaiah, receive your own vision and a personal coal of fire for your lips so that you can worship and praise God in truth and help spread the good news of Christ to all!

Dying, seeing hell, and then returning back to life affected me, traumatized me.

Experiencing heaven fixed that. I found peace with God when He allowed me to see heaven.

* * *

Night Ryder: "Welcome back! We have B.W. Melvin back with us. He has an amazing testimony on heaven! That's a far cry from experiencing hell like we heard last time. What a testimony!

"But before we begin, while folks are joining the show tonight, there are questions we were discussing before we aired that I would like our listeners to hear because it sets the stage for how heaven should affect the modern church so that God's will would be done on earth as it is in heaven as Matthew 6:10 says!"

"That's right," Tina replied. "Before the show, we were discussing why churches here in the United States do not see miracles like we saw overseas recently during a missions trip. Overseas we've seen healings, dramatic answers to prayer, God working through people, His gifts, and radical transformative salvations occur in abundance. Yet here in America, there is so little."

"That's right, Tina," Night Ryder said. "It seems people here in the States have been programmed to discount any supernatural acts of God—even life after death accounts or seeing heaven like Isaiah or Ezekiel did. We were discussing why. Brian, since we are now in pre-show, would you tell us your interesting perspective on this topic?"

"Yes, Night Ryder, Tina. Heaven gives you an eternal perspective on things, more respect for God, and a sense of responsibility that seems to be lacking in much of modern-day America and western churches where content is largely based on evangelism and their marketing strategies. Not only that, but there exists a focus on 'hyper intellectualism' about all things Christian rather than faith in God and His word."

Tina interjected, "Now folks, we are not speaking bad about all churches, but for so many, after being overseas and returning here, I can't help but seeing churches as divided and hype-focused."

"Seeing heaven gives you the same perspective, Tina," I replied.

* * *

As I listened to Tina, I thought about how Americans were so influenced by image and form. Keeping up with those images or forms requires marketing. The whitest teeth, the best product, all for you. Nothing negative allowed as that spoils the image of the product being sold. We have a skewed perspective because our eyes are on self rather than Christ. Our eyes should be on Christ. We were made in the image of God, of Christ. Should we look at Christ for our identity, for our image and form, we would be moved by what we see and the world would be moved by seeing Christ in us.

This skewed vision hinders the western church. The result is that many do not experience the miracles that happen overseas. There, people are moved by God's Spirit, masses are saved, and many healings are accounted for. But here—well, not so much.

What we have instead is image with no substance. Gates of hell knocking against our walls. *Shhhh, don't say that—that's negative, brother!*

In the Bible, gates represented places where judgments, laws, and all the happenings in a kingdom were decreed and carried out. My, how the gates of the world infect the church with their ways today.

It is we, the church, who should be storming the enemy's gates, not the other way around. However, whitewash is cheaper. No getting out of the boat necessary. Whitewash is not offensive!

In the Bible we see nothing was covered over. Human nature is exposed raw, warts and all. Consider King David and his family, or Hagar and Sarah, or the rebellious children of Israel. Throughout the Bible, God called people to return to Him to be healed. Oh, the great faithfulness of God!

How different that is from modern western churches, where it is all about image and form, like having the best music and light shows and the hippest and coolest ministers agreeing with the dictates of culture. Those in the audience are forgotten. Their broken hearts are not healed. People remain enslaved in recurring sins. Others are bound in their personal mental prisons and find very little hope of release. But at least the church puts on good shows. People come, but sadly, many leave as broken as when they came. Thankfully, there are a few churches that do what they can to help people be set free.

Amidst this are people who have gotten so used to their personal misery; they do not recognize or seek to be free from their wounds. They use their personal misery or drama for the purpose of getting attention or to feel wanted. They simply do not know any other way to assuage the deep emptiness they feel. What can you do when, in so many places, feelings and problems are swept under the rug? Many churches are more concerned with image and form, so issues are not dealt with. The focus is not on counselors and healing but rather activities.

They ignore the words from Isaiah 61:1-4 and John 16:7 where the Holy Spirit is our helper so we can give good news to those crushed by life, help heal the broken heart, and set the oppressed free. Yet thank God for those who at least try doing what they can in these matters.

God is all about proclaiming good news to those crushed in spirit, about healing broken and wounded hearts, giving liberty to those held captive, and setting those bound inside their personal prisons free from rejection, betrayal, neglect, effects of abuse, abandonment, bitterness, addictions, religious spirits, pride, and the list goes on and on.

God's power from heaven changes those poor and crushed in spirit with the gospel message of Jesus Christ and with His personal presence. In the process of the journey, they get their hearts mended and sight restored. "*Thy Kingdom come, thy will be done in earth, as it is in heaven,*" Jesus said in Matthew 6:10 (KJV). Why we see so little of God moving in great ways in the west, in my opinion, is because many are simply not taught about God's faithfulness to us, His beloved children.

* * *

Tina injected, "Yes, that's what we have seen overseas, a trust in God's faithfulness. For many, there is no other way than to trust in the sovereign nature of God."

"Instead, here in the States," Night Ryder responded, "it seems to me that many churches have become places where weird things go on like dancing in a conga line to catch imagery dollars dropping from heaven, fake healings, and all those manipulative appeals for money. Also, there are those who market God's great faithfulness and promises only as the means to get what you need or want. I've also seen other places use a cold, dry rationalism to explain how God, who is unchanging and reneges on no gift or calling, somehow did so because the spiritual gifts are longer valid today."

Tina chimed in, "Overseas, we've seen these in action, for real, but here in the States, I've witnessed people chirping like chickens and barking like dogs being passed off as being filled with the spirit."

"A dry rationalism sinks in, where the love and grace of God are removed. A dry formalism takes over. Or the goal is being right at all costs, so much so that the church remains fragmented, divided. People are tired of this. Oh, Jesus, only You can fix this mess!"

"Yes," I replied, "Only Jesus can fix this mess because He is faithful."

CHAPTER THREE

TWELVE HOURS BEFORE HEAVEN

"The Lord looks from heaven; He sees all the sons of men."
—Psalm 33:13 NKJV

Have you ever had days when everything that could go wrong does? Is this all there is to the Christian life? I thought, *Wasn't it all to be roses and blessings instead? Where are the flowers—all I get are thorns!* Have you ever felt that way?

Back in the day, I had a 1981 blue Nissan truck. As I was pulling into Ed's Diner at 3 p.m. on a Sunday afternoon, Tom was waiting for me. He was one crazy, newly converted Christian. He still loved alcohol a bit too much, which gave him the courage to preach to anyone not wanting to hear. My mission was to disciple him and help him quit his boozing ways. That was one of my many works back in the day. Part of being the body of Christ, you know. I never realized I too had mud in my own eyes on my way to the healing waters.

"Geez, Tom, you been drinking again," I said as I got out of my truck. "We're supposed to go to church. What the heck…"

"I am ready to go. PRAISE THE LORD!" shouted Tom, "I just had a few beers, a meal would do me good. I'll buy. Can't wait to meet your pastor..."

Holy kosher hot dogs, this promises to be some night! I thought.

We were headed to Holy Tabernacle pastored by the Rev. Ron Loos, a man who loved to talk and talk! Holy Tabernacle was unlike most churches; it was a "going church." The members met together more than once a week and fellowshipped with each other daily. We were like one big extended family who loved God.

Pastor Ron Loos and his wife brought about a unique camaraderie at ol' Holy Tabernacle that I have rarely seen since. Every member had a sense of purpose through their inspired messages, sermons, and tireless counseling teams. Looking back on this now, I realize this was unique. We were a Christian community and not the typical diners-club variety of church with its endless special-effect shows, hype, and chatter that agrees with the world more than the Bible.

Holy Tabernacle was nearing the end of a string of stirring revival meetings held over a long weekend. This particular Sunday was the last night. I had to be there early to set up the sound. Now, with Tom drunk and going to meet Pastor Loos, what could one do?

During this time, I involved myself in many things so I could keep the trauma of experiencing hell out of my mind. I never wanted to go back there. So I ran the sound board and was part of the praise band. Pastor Ron also volunteered me to be the head intercessor of the church. On top of all this, I was involved in discipleship and leadership training. In my spare time, I started a small cleaning business on the side. Looking back, I didn't have much time to myself. I spent my week going to work and street witnessing to lost youth in the evenings. I was busier than a bee amidst a bouquet of spring flowers in early June.

The waitress seated us. The coffee special at ten cents a cup would come in real handy! I drank 50 cents worth of coffee. This promised to be a long night. Tom was chomping away on a steak and between bites said we forgot to pray before our meal. We stopped and bowed our heads, but before I could quietly pray, Tom was moved by the Spirit:

"Oh, dear Lordy, forgive us for not praying before this THY HOLY meal and bless this food and the LOVELY STEAK AS TOUGH AS SHOE LEATHER to the nourishment of our bodies. And, Holy Lord of all Creation, see these SINNERS sitting NEXT TO US AND ALL IN THIS PLACE. LET THEM EACH COME TO JESUS AND BECOME BORN AGAIN so HELLFIRE won't ruin their next meal and burn their steak too. AMEN and oh my! Let's eat!"

I wanted to crawl under the table as people glared back at us, shaking their heads with disparagement dancing in their eyes. You could read their minds: *Christians!*

Tom finished eating as though nothing was wrong. He began preaching loudly to the waitress, and when she said she was a Christian, he asked for her phone number and a date. She gave him a number. When Tom proudly showed me, I dared not tell him it was the number for dial-a-prayer. Tom, true to his word, paid the bill. Turning to Tom, I told him I'd meet him outside after I used the restroom and freshened up. Five cups of coffee, you know. Tom slapped me on the back and went outside. A mistake, coffee. Wow this was going to be a long night!

Outside, I found Tom standing in the back of my truck smoking a joint! With each puff, he cried out as loudly as he could, "PRAISE THE LORD! GLORY TO GOD FOR THE HERBS OF THE GROUND! HEY, ALL YOU SINNERS, REPENT FOR THE KINGDOM IS AT HAND!"

"Tom!" I yelled disapprovingly. "What the hay are you doing?"

Taking a long hit on the joint, Tom replied, "Enjoying the herbs of the Lord. And all you people out there, Jesus is coming again—THE RAPTURE IS AT HAND! I feel moved by the Spirit. Yee-haw…"

With this Tom flicked the small burning end of the joint into a wash culvert nearby. *Great shot—the police will probably be here soon,* I thought to myself, *and me a respectable young member of the hippest church in town.*

"Tom, what am I going to do? You'll be meeting the pastor of my church and in your condition what will he think of you?"

"Ah, don't worry—I'll straighten out! Praise the Lord! I is a first-time visitor and only been saved one month ago to the day, hallelujah! Celebrating, that's all! I love Jesus!"

"Get in the truck, Tom, let's go…"

Tom climbed in the passenger seat smelling like a smoldering rope factory. I began to worry. *What will people think, seeing me with such a person as this!*

Rolling down Main Street heading toward church, Tom stuck his head out the car window singing hymns as loudly as he could and telling anyone seen walking to "get saved today as it is better to turn than to burn."

Why me, Lord, why me?

How would God's love act in such a scene—as a Pharisee or patient saint?

God tests us all the time. How has He tested you? What do you need to be healed of that is delaying heaven's power to set you free?

Tonight was the last night of four days of fiery revival meetings with baptisms every night. Here I was driving with a stoned convert. I began wishing there was someone else to run the sound system, do intercessory prayer group, set up and cue in the band, and get the pastor's mic set. *Where's the closest rock I could crawl under?*

This promised to be a super-late Sunday evening service. *I may not get home till dawn*, I angrily thought. *I'll be lucky if I make it home by midnight. Heck, I gotta get up at 5 in the morning to boot, geez, and get to work.*

"Hey Bry ol' buddy, don't worry Jezus loves you. Hey everybody, Jezus set me freez! Yea ha waa hooo ie…"

* * *

"This is Night Ryder on ZWTW Christian radio's 'Evening Talk.' We were discussing what makes a church a church."

Tina interposed, "Speaking about churches, when we left off, we were talking about how so many Christians get so busy with doing churchy things, they seem to be missing the real reason why there is church. Why do you think that is, Bryan?"

"Well, for starters, I did churchy things so I would not have time to feel alone. I thought that if I worked hard enough, I could avoid the risk of not doing enough for God. At that time, I was hiding from myself by erecting a façade of busyness, a veneer. I think many Christians often do the same in many ways."

"Yes, that's a fact for almost the whole human race," Tina chimed in. "People seem to like to avoid feeling alone, or they have a need to feel accepted, so they busy themselves."

"Or bury themselves in iPads, iPhones, computers, texting, and tweeting, so there is no sense of rejection," Night Ryder added, "unless defriended or canceled."

"Often modern church can take the form of broadcasting some grand vision and then holding fantastic meetings with the hottest praise music in town and, finally, topping it off with some 45-plus-year-old non-offending hipster pastors in skinny jeans selling lattes in the lobby," I added.

"Yep, that's right. People are lost in endless activities. I've noticed it too," Tina replied. "You know, when the context is right, these things are okay and serve a purpose for God, I'm sure. Some folks get help and are saved!

"Now, I am not bad-mouthing the church for having programs, clubs, and events," I said, "but when there isn't much else, is it any wonder so many folks no longer want to go to church?"

"Yes," said Tina, "some of the things, Ryder, we all saw on the mission trip to Africa, such as healings, changed lives, casting devils out of people, makes it seem like something's missing in the States, the West, so people drop out."

"And they are missing something!" Night Ryder interjected. "Latest polls and studies show how people of all ages are falling out of church. Some churches make a new Jesus in the image of their culture in order to attract people, while other places are too intellectual to the detriment of their faith. So folks drop out."

CHAPTER FOUR

TEN HOURS BEFORE HEAVEN

"For by grace you have been saved through faith...not of works."

—Ephesians 2:8-9 NKJV

Pulling into the church parking lot was a relief. *No police.* Holy Tabernacle was one of the fastest-growing churches in town in the early 1980s. Rev. Ron E. Loos hailed from Georgia and came to Colorado to pastor a once-small church of 40 souls.

After he came, the numbers swelled to 300 and were still growing. We were a "happening church" as the church logo said: "Spirit filled and Holy Ghost led—Holy Tabernacle is the place you are fed."

What's all this appeal for food? We Christians must be a hungry lot!

Since I was running the sound board, I had to be early to get things set up. Service would begin at 6 p.m. The band would drift in a little after 5 p.m. and set up. By that time, I had to have all the microphones ready to go and pre-adjusted per singer. Tom was okay, sitting quietly reading his Bible, until he spied the drum set.

The sanctuary, along with its balcony, was set in a semi-circle fashion. The sound board was in the middle of the back row. The stage was elevated three steps above the floor. The drum set was a permanent fixture on stage. Tom looked up and said, "Wow a Holy-o drum'oo Tabernacle set!"

Tom took a beeline straight to the drums and began to play the worst imitation of the longest Led Zeppelin drum solo ever heard. Pastor Ron came out of his office upstairs and looked down from the balcony at me and Tom. I could not hear what Pastor Ron was yelling. Tom stopped and said, "Nice drums!"

Pastor Ron yelled down, "Hey, nice job, maybe someday you'll be a rock star, but please keep it down a bit. I need to get ready for the evening. Bryan, is this a friend of yours...I see?"

I noticed how he said *I see* with that grin.

"Yes, this is Tom—he wanted to check out the church." I felt small and embarrassed, and I was hoping the pastor would not come downstairs and get a whiff of Tom's smoky rope and stale booze aroma. *What would he think of me? Hmmm, I see—friend of yours!*

"Hi Tom, glad you are here. Maybe you would like to be baptized tonight?"

"Amen, maybe—where's the tank?"

"Behind the upper curtain behind the stage—water is being filled now. I'll turn it off in a few minutes. Praise God that you could come, Tom."

With this Pastor Ron smiled, waved, and walked toward his office. Quickly turning, he looked right at me, chuckling, "One of yours, Bryan...that figures."

"Tom, help me cue the mics before the band gets here."

That was a mistake. A microphone in the hands of an inebriated person who thinks he can croon like Waylon Jennings on a hot Saturday night. *Oh my!*

The band arrived. Tom settled down and sat near the sound booth singing blue grass hymns quietly to himself while absent-mindedly flipping through a pew-edition Bible.

Tylor was a very talented drummer and singer. He was also the praise and worship leader as well as the church's resident theologian. However, if you did not meet his theological standards, you could not play in the band. We had standards back then. You had to be a Christian who reads the Bible to be part of the band, not some unsaved hayseed from the local bar who could play a good lick.

I enjoyed discussing theology and philosophy with Taylor along with the piano player, Craig, the resident psychology student from Colorado State. Tyler was the only married person in the band; the rest were college-aged singles looking for their own prospective mates. After all, what are church "singles, college, and career" groups for? *Be honest now!*

Both guitar players were good. So was the bass player. John played rhythm and was filling in for me that night as we switched back and forth to run the sound system. Larry played bass and Rich was the lead. We all enjoyed talking Bible shop and making sure theology was correct and correcting any error with long opines.

The girls in the band were called the "Amen Sisters." The Amen Sisters were not related but earned this honored title for sitting in the front row shouting, "*Amen!* Preach it, pastor."

Jill, Stacie, and Marla made up this trio. They sang in unison in a snappy rhythm and blues accompaniment to Tyler's singing. All were clapping hands and jiving with the beat enough to make a single man rather hot around the collar if the truth be known.

I was adjusting the sound for each person's voice. Blending these with the instruments to sound good takes talent. For some odd reason, only I could do this to Pastor Ron's specifications. Jason sat next to me learning the board while waiting for pastor's approval for his big day online.

Running the sound board was a hoot. I had a set of headphones on and could switch to each singer and hear them alone. Only Tyler could really sing, belt it all out in pitch and key. The gals, well, you had to set the highs and lows just right.

The Amen Sisters had to be blended. Jill sang so soft I had to set her gain on high, tone down the base to -2, raise the mid to +3, treble 0, and she sounded great. Marla was the belter of songs and sang way too loudly—gain on soft, +4 mid, negative base at -5, and treble at +1. Fade the rest.

Stacie had the voice that only a mother could love. Midrange adjustment with settings at -1 worked for her. Blended together, the "Sisters" sounded great. *I just hope they will not switch mics during the service!* Stacie had her eye on John and had a habit of looking at him longingly and switching microphones during their R&B dance routines to get closer to him. This often caused her to miss coming in on time—mute button or a quick fade worked well for this.

How would God's love act in such a scene—a Pharisee or patient saint? God tests us all the time. How has He been testing you? Can't you see heaven's power at work in times like this?

The band cued up and practiced a few songs. By then the early arrivals were coming in. Sure enough, Mary and Bob walked in. They were young high schoolers and had been dating for a few years. Bob and Mary were sweethearts and had a bad habit of kissing nonstop while entwined in each other's arms during the services at Holy Tabernacle. Sure enough, they sat close to me and began hugging and kissing. *What's a poor sound man to do?* Telling them to stop only caused the kissing to intensify and the noise!

What a church! Many of the parishioners were devout Christians sprinkled haphazardly among the codependent wounded masses. We had a convicted felon who had been recently released from prison on a technicality and was now dating a schoolteacher. There were various homeless folks fresh off the streets who visited daily, expecting the usual freebees and handouts.

There were the rich and the poor all mingled together in the pews. People from all walks of life congregated to hear the word of God, because, *Holy Tabernacle—Spirit filled, Holy Ghost led, the place where you are fed!*

What a church! There were young, old, the pretty and not very pretty, and just plain folks with plenty of warts and all. It was a counselor's nightmare. Pastor Ron and his lovely wife, Barb, sure had their hands full.

Barb held a women's Bible study that was bursting with new members. Pastor Ron sure could teach amazingly from the word of God. It was all ablaze in activities and endless ministry opportunities. It was a church on the go, all abuzz. Amazingly, looking back, Ron Loos actually trained us well in how to look after each other. The power of the Holy Spirit was at work revealing our warts and healing our flaws through each other. I definitely needed a lot of mine removed, that's for sure!

One of the ushers, Dolan, came in. He was a recovering heroin addict on methadone. While singing loudly during praise and worship, ol' Dolan passed out, fell straight back with a hard thud on the floor. Everyone looked, smiled, clapped, sang, and thought he was slain in the Spirit, lying on the floor exactly as he had fallen, arms outstretched with the biggest of all, happy grins on his face.

An elderly couple spoke up to their friends, "Look, he must be seeing a vision…"

"Must be see'n the Lord! G-GLORY BE!"

"Amen! Hallelujah!" the church shouted as old man Walker leaped over Dolan and began dancing like King David did, clothed though, twirling his suit jacket over his head. The band was rocking that night!

There was Dolan, flat-out, grinning ear to ear in happy land. Yep, those of us who knew him knew better and were ready for CPR just in case. Those were crazy times, each second filled with the grace of God that slowly transformed our lives.

Some churches can be more exciting than a Texas bar on Friday night after payday, and other times, as pleasant as a spring breeze. I even heard some people opine that some churches, well, sort of smell like formaldehyde.

Despite all this, I was in a crabby and foul mood, mostly because I was weary, worn, and tired. I needed to put on my best Jesus face and play the role. Faithfully I was fulfilling my church duties in hopes I'd please the Lord. *Grrrr…chores…*

The goal of our happening sing'n and shout'n and praise'n Jesus church was to save souls. However, had any one of us ever bothered to ask what you do with them after you caught 'em for Jesus, all saved, pleasantly stuffed, and knowledge fed?

We had no clue other than have more meetings, more activities, new believer classes, aerobic classes, Bible studies, accountability meetings, Greek and Hebrew language classes, hang out after church in a restaurant, more Bible classes, discipleship workshops, or head to this or that Christian seminar to hear the latest and greatest sermons in the world, and then on to another restaurant.

Not that any of this was drastically wrong. Yet like veneer, it kept us from seeing the personal healing and wholeness that needed to happen. Hearts needed to be healed. It was like all the activities provided a smoke screen to hide behind, because we really didn't know what more to do. We substituted knowing God with knowing things, doing things, and eating.

The only time I felt like I was reaching God, really getting to know Him, was when I was on the street witnessing or in the intercessory prayer group Pastor Loos volunteered me to lead. I felt the closest when I was praying for another person.

Then it was back to all these activities all over and over and over again! I began to think, *Is this all there is to this Christianity thing?*

Ever thought the same?

CHAPTER FIVE

THE CALLER

"He pled the cause of the afflicted and needy; then it was well. Is not that what it means to know Me?' declares the Lord."

— Jeremiah 22:16 NASB

"This is Night Ryder; the phone lines are lighting up about our discussion on churches. Go ahead, Jack from Olympia, Washington. Top of the day to you, Jack!"

"Thank you for taking my call! I am glad you all are speaking about churches; I know there are no perfect ones. We need good Bible teaching, programs, and all that, but I am feeling a bit burned out on these things. So my question has to do more with—what is church for?

I replied, "That's a good question, Jack. The church is called the bride of Christ and is made up of believers who should be learning how to become the hands and feet, the body, of Christ. Let's make it simple—the church has three functions. There is the hospital phase, the rehabilitation and training phase, and the embarkation phase."

"Hmmm, interesting—like a hospital?" Tina responded.

"Yes, a place where wounded souls, battered and bruised by life, can safely go to be healed. A good church needs many good spiritual doctors and nurses, with lots of patients. What did Jesus say in Luke 4, quoting from Isaiah 61:1-4?"

Jack answered, "Wow, I just read that earlier today! He said to preach good news to the poor in spirit, heal the broken hearts, set at liberty those who are bound, recover the sight of the blind, set at liberty those who are oppressed. Proclaim what is acceptable to the Lord.

"Isaiah 61 adds to warn of the vengeance of God and to comfort and console those who sorrow. Basically, reveal Jesus to them so that they resurrect out of sorrow, heaviness, out of sin's control and learn to rebuild newness of life, no longer living in the ashes of the past—or something like that."

"Yes, you got that right," I replied. "This comes by the new birth. The power of the indwelling Holy Spirit takes up residence inside us and begins the process of becoming His body on earth, like God's hospital to a sick and dying world."

Night Ryder spoke up, "A hospital is a good description of a church and its functions. Is that what you are saying, Bryan?"

"Yes, this hospital in a nutshell involves God's healing grace that changes us inside out. You can't earn grace, because in a hospital room you are at the merciful healing hands of the Great Physician and His assistants. Surgery, wound care, treatment, and being nursed back to health are part of the hospital phase.

"After the hospital phase, you enter the rehab/training phase where you learn 'new creation' life skills. You learn what it means to walk the walk and talk and talk by staying true to the Bible. It is here you move on into the internship phase as assistants of the Great Physician."

"This is called discipleship," interrupted the caller.

"Yes, discipleship, like a hospital internship. Here, you learn to practice being the hands and feet, the body, of Christ working together as a skilled medical team, healing, mending, and maturing those drawn by the Father into your local assembly."

Jack: "Are you a Calvinist?"

Wow, where did that come from?

"No, I am not," I answered and continued.

"From the intern phase, you are ready to embark as a skilled EMT into a hurting world as the hands and feet of the body of Christ. You bring the wounded lives into 'Great Physician Hospital' where you pass the torch of your Holy Spirit-learned skills on to future generations" (see 2 Corinthians 1:4).

"Wow," exclaimed Tina, "Church is where you spend time in the recovery room of grace. After that, move on to the rehabilitation phase, learning new creation life skills, to enter into the internship following the Great Physician and His staff around!"

"That's right," I responded, "You develop your personal specialist skills as part of His team. Some become EMT paramedics, others become evangelists, others are administrators, and others still are assistants or helpers. Get the picture?"

"Yes, I do!" said Jack.

"Think of it," I continued. "You begin to see folks coming in with their wounded, battered souls, lost in their egos, escape the dreariness of life, seeking to find acceptance and purpose here on planet Earth.

"Their woundedness drives them to act the way they do. To quote a famous counselor, 'Hurt people hurt people, but healed people heal people.' For example, some folks lack intimacy and relationships so they immerse themselves in pornography to compensate. Others feel rejection or loneliness and drown their pain in drugs and alcohol. Many exhibit power and control mechanisms to cover feelings of insecurity and fear of rejection. The prescription for all this heart sickness is a deeper relationship with their creator who loves and cares for them. Also, knowing the word, God's truth and His order, replaces the lies that have crept into their lives.

"A majority of folks even self-sabotage and bring pain to those around them, and most sadly, pass the lies and pain on to their children. You see, folks are taken captive to all kinds of disappointments, disorder, and lies; they fill the spiritual Emergency Room, the church, awaiting encounters from the one Doctor who can bring truth and hope to broken and hurting hearts. The church should be God's community helping to heal their wounds by bringing them to the Doctor who calls to them, just like when Jesus called to Lazarus, and he was raised from the dead.

"Hurting people can come back to life as their lies and pain are unbound so they actually encounter the Great Physician, His truth, and His love. They learn great provision through Jesus and life with His Holy Spirit who indwells us. The church community stands by us and brings us to a place of encountering the Great Physician as we are unbound.

"All people have problems, in and out of church. But when we, the staff and any and all of God's disciples, bring people to Jesus, the Holy Spirit gently exposes those misbeliefs about themselves and about God to their heart. We encounter Him through His Holy Spirit, His unbounding grace and mercy, which heals our hearts and brings Him glory."

Tina interrupted, "What you mention, Bryan, reminds me of the parable of the Good Samaritan. Battered souls beaten by robbers on life's highway. People pass by, more concerned about their own image and needs. Jesus comes along, picks us up, and pours on the healing wine and oil. He carries us to the inn—the church—where He charges the innkeepers." (All are sinners and fall short of God's glory, even the innkeepers. Through the community of the church, we help one another be accountable continually.)

"You mean church staff! That's good!" Night Ryder exclaimed. "Jesus provides the means for the care of the wounded soul, and then in His faithfulness pays the cost upon His return like the Good Samaritan" (see Luke 10:35).

"Wow," Jack said, rather nervously.

"Into this mix, the Lord places folks into a church community so we can be healed, grow, learn, and then embark on becoming the plantings of the Lord, helping to resurrect those around us out of their darkness into the brand-new life that John 3:16 talks about."

"I wish all churches were like that," said Tina, "a place of healing from the hurts of life. You know, so often they're not. It's difficult to reveal our weaknesses to others.

Jack: "Yes, I tried and was, well, told to do this or that. No one listened—so I wore my best Jesus mask."

"Me too," I replied. "It is easy to join a bandwagon and sit in any congregation, thump yourself upon the chest saying we have great music and messages, we even honor all feast days, keep the Sabbath to the letter, but if that's all one does—all veneer…"

Tina interrupted, "Yes, we build grand buildings for God, and that's fine up to a point—due to necessity, mind you—but recall how the religious leaders of Jesus' day were rebuked for hiding behind the law while neglecting the weightier matters of the greatest law of all, the law for them and for us today—grace. Love. Even discipline."

Night Ryder interjected, "For many, our churches are becoming less and less new creation life rehabilitation centers…"

Jack: "...or a hospital mending the broken heart..."

Tina: "...equipping the poor in spirit with true Holy Ghost strength or declaring to those held captive how they can be released from those things that are ruining their lives!"

I responded, "Or helping them encounter the Lord so they can be set free from their mental prisons of fear, rejection, abandonment, neglect, abuse. All this takes time while God works through the mess, but in the end healing comes. By this, no matter how wacky a church is, God supernaturally works in ways we do not see, slowly helping all. The closer or better we know Jesus and experience His grace and mercy, the more we become healed. It is not us or the staff who heals; it is Jesus.

"Jesus reflected the Father, and we will bring glory to God as we are healed and able to reflect His mercy and grace to others. That's when He is glorified. This comes by knowing Him more and more each passing day. How do we get there?

"I can only answer for myself, but it's by a life of getting quiet so we can hear His voice as we meditate on His word. And also, by being mindful that He is with us at all times so we can attribute everything and all things to Him. We can reflect back our gratitude. The Bible supernaturally transforms our lives; we learn about Him, and we get to encounter Him" (see Colossians 1:9-13).

"As for prayer, after experiencing heaven, this prayer helped me the most:

"Dear Lord Jesus, help me to see through Your eyes of grace and endure what I see. Change me and teach me Your ways so I become a better reflection of You."

Do you remember when Jesus healed the man who could only see people vaguely, like trees? In the same way, sometimes our eyes need a second touch from the Lord so we can see others with eyes full of grace and mercy the way Jesus sees them.

CHAPTER SIX

EIGHT HOURS BEFORE HEAVEN

"For I desire steadfast love and not sacrifice, the knowledge of God rather than burnt offerings."

—Hosea 6:6 ESV

People streamed into ol' Holy Tabernacle. I recall Nick, the resident salesman who had all the latest Christian weight-loss plans, diet supplements, and fantastic healthy juice drinks anybody could ever need.

"Hey Bryan, I have some new seaweed liver invigorator capsules that will help a person have that extra energy and get up and go."

"No thanks, Nick, I use coffee."

Madison heard Nick. "Oh Nick, really? I love that almond, ginseng, ginger paste; I am down another five pounds! What's this you have now?"

Off they went to the side and soon a small crowd gathered around old Nick. Tyler by the door began welcoming everyone to come on in. Let the praise begin!

Where is Tom? Amidst all the commotion, I lost track of Tom! There was a loud splash and someone yelling behind the deep red curtains covering the baptistry.

The music stopped. Brief silence

"Ahhh, that's cold! Hallelujah! Splish splash I've taken a bath—on a Sunday night! Yea, baptized in the name of the Lord—whoo hooo!"

I found Tom. You could hear the water being flailed about. Big wet spots were appearing on the curtains. A little boy nearby yanked on his mother's sleeve and excitedly yelled, "They have a pool, they have a pool! Can I go swimming, Mommy? *Pleeease?* I wanna, I wanna!"

Pastor Loos ran back to the baptistry. In the excitement, someone hit the switch to the electric baptistry curtains by mistake. The motors hummed; the red veils slowly opened. There was Tom, bare chested, singing "How Great Thou Art."

Pastor Ron had his cordless mic on, speaking to the usher, "That's Bryan's friend…"

People looked at me. I read their unified expression—*that figures.* Pastor Ron without thought stepped down into the baptismal pool. So much for the fine suit.

"Praise God! Looks like we'll get started early folks. One person was in a hurry to get ahead of the line—this is Tom. He wants to be first. So be it then, brother."

Tom was obviously stoned. Pastor Ron recovered really well. People began sitting down. The band and the Amen Sisters did not know what to do other than stare at Tom.

Pastor Loos was finding it difficult not to laugh. The audience could only see mid-waist high. The usher could be heard muffling his laughter. Made me wonder what we in the crowd could not see. Well, maybe best not to know.

"Tom, do you hereby make a profession of faith and swear to stay off liquor and drugs, go back to school, and get a job as evidence of making Jesus Lord of your life?"

"I'ze most certainly dooo de do!"

"Therefore, be baptized in the name of the Father…"

Pastor Ron, holding Tom, dunked him joyfully in the water. Raising him up, Tom yelled, "WOWEE! That's cold!"

"In the name of the Son, Jesus Christ…"

Pastor submerged him again, holding him a few seconds longer than before. Tom came out of the water shouting, *"I feel the Spirit!"*

The congregation went wild, shouting praises to God and clapping in approval: *He's feeling the Spirit. Praise the Lord. Glory brother. God bless you.*

"And in the name of the Holy Spirit…"

Third dunk was the charm. Tom came out of the water a new man singing like Johnny Cash, *"I saw the light…"*

A new man on a mission, Tom leaped upon the stairs leading out of the baptismal pool. All anyone noticed was water-laden white boxer shorts adorned with little red hearts. The rear sagged a bit as well.

Luckily the vision was brief as someone wrapped a blanket around his shoulders. *He came with Bryan, ohhh…*

"Tom, brother, you are now baptized in the name of Jesus." Pastor Loos bellowed, "Welcome to the kingdom of God! Tyler! *Strike up the band! One sinner who repents causes the host of heaven to sing—let's all join in!"*

With this the Amen Sisters began clapping and dancing around microphones in perfect choreography. Pastor Ron could be seen going back up the stairs to his office to change into dry pants, trailing a stream of water behind.

An usher was wringing out a mop bucket to clean up the residue. *Nice recovery.* Tom later came out to the front row. No more smell of rope. He was the darling of the evening. I thought it odd—the pastor usually only dunked once, not three times.

Tyler crooned popular praise choruses and the Amen Sisters jived around. Adjusting and blending the sound was easy. The parishioners were singing, some raising their hands to the Lord, others dancing, all getting into the music and praising the Lord again.

Tom was up front dancing and singing loudest of all. Mary and Bob were still kissing. *How could they do this? In church no less! Can't they come up for air?*

The music flowed and ebbed into slow worship. Pastor Ron came back out on stage wearing new, light brown pants. Tom danced around the front row like a rap singer doing a war dance.

"Praise God, I see Tom is *surely* filled tonight!" cried out Pastor Ron.

The church clapped noisily and hollered with approval. Tom stopped his dance, looked up, and was beaming.

"Brother, you can sit now and rest in the Lord!"

Tom smiled and waved to the crowd and sat down on the front row. Everyone else sat down too. I had to admire Pastor Ron handling this situation with finesse. If only the people knew how lit Tom was. All I could think about was that afterward I would hear disapproval about all this from Pastor Ron Loos, but I never did. That was pure grace.

Pastor Ron began the sermon with a short prayer and began to teach: "Tonight, we baptize many here into the kingdom of God! Placing them into the body of Christ for resurrection and new life. Old things will pass away, and all things begin new. Right, Tom?"

Tom shouted loudly, "Amen AND AMEN!"

"Before we begin the baptisms, let me share with you from the Bible about the bride of Christ—His church, His bride."

Something caught Pastor's eye. He gave a quick three second stare-down and said, "Hey Bob, Mary, up there in the back. Bob—you willin' to take Mary as your bride? You two do need to come up for air soon. After all, this is church."

Mary looked at Bob. "Oh, Bob—married? Oh! Yes...I do!"

All I could think was, *Oh brother, is this church the bride of Christ?*

Dolan was lying on the floor again, grinning ear to ear and once in a while letting out a giggle and sigh. Slain in the Spirit, they say—*hmmm.*

Bob looked at Mary, and from where I sat, I thought they would commence where they left off, but Bob replied, "First thing after high school, kitten cakes."

The crowd roared with approving laughter and clapping. For the first time in a long time, these two sat listening to the entire sermon. You had to admire the skill of Pastor Ron.

"Now, people of God—you and I, we together—are the church, the bride of Christ. Do you know what this means? Can a person live like the bride and still live like the world?"

Quiet gasps mixed with a few loud amens resounded in the room. Pastor Ron continued:

"Jesus in Matthew 25:1-13 tells of five wise and five foolish bridesmaids waiting for the bridegroom. Their mission: prepare the bride for the bridegroom. We see here, Jesus is telling us to be wise and prepare the bride before Christ comes calling for His church to arise with Him. Don't be foolish—be wise!

"Are you one preparing the bride for heaven, or are you 'foolish'—asleep in the world, hiding behind a smoke screen of religion while neglecting the weightier matters of what grace is about, as Titus 2:11-15 helps define it?

"Just like Matthew 25, those foolish bridesmaids thought they had enough oil but burned it all up on their own desires rather than being the hands, feet, and body of Christ."

Looking back at all this, I have noticed that there is not much of this style of preaching today. Most nowadays are self-help sermons because, after all, self-improvement sells and keeps people coming back for more. Then one's oil runs dry listening to sales pitches for a "healthier, prosperous you."

Pastor Loos kept folks riveted when he preached:

"In Revelation 2 and 3 we discover that five of the seven churches needed to repent while two did not. Maybe the five churches are people in the church living in the last days who are like the five foolish bridesmaids before Christ's coming. The contexts of these chapters are the same—the end times just before Jesus returns.

"Let's see, the first foolish bridesmaid is like those folks in that Ephesus assembly who left their first love. Their flame dimed. No oil. Why? They were the holy nitpickers, browbeaters, legalists, and heresy hunters of the church. Their keen eyes are sorely needed, but when their love is all about browbeating and hunting heretics, things sour.

"These Ephesus types forget what it means to be governed by God's love and instead find fault with everybody. What they say rules. This defines their love for God. They need to get a refill of oil. I pray some do, but I fear most choose to sleep in illusions of grandeur of being the only right ones in the entire church world. They need oil! Holy Spirit repentance, return to your first love!"

Looking around the congregation, I spied ol' Willis Bean, the chief complainer in the church and special critic of Pastor Loos, shouting *amen* loudly in his pew.

"Then there are the Pergamos-type bridesmaids who compromise with the world and justify mixing the new age occult into the church because they reason the devil stole the formulas for success from God, so we can use the same occult formulas to get our gifts from God. Really?

"These Pergamos types are into power trips, lording their titles over others while asleep at the foot of Satan's throne, getting the latest revelation by both teaching and prophesying half-truths baited with lies, thinking they are helping the church.

"Their fire is going out. They need to turn away from corrupting the church or else the Lord will fight against them with the sword of His mouth seen in Revelation 19."

I heard someone near me quietly talking to another and handing them a book about *Visualize Prosperity God's Way in Ten Easy Steps.*

"Another foolish bridesmaid is lulled to sleep by doctrines. The Thyatira types want to control the world, make a kingdom for themselves to control. They allow that Jezebel spirit to prophesy that we need to take over the world first and hand it over to Jesus on a silver platter; only then can He return as they prophesied."

There was Brandon Major who was big on mixing religion into politics to take control of the media, arts, entertainment, government, military, news, and business world. I don't think he understood that concept came from the occult world.

"Oh, the Sardis bridesmaids of the church are asleep, never doing anything. They were too lazy to get any oil. They are ecumenical, like the world. Teach a soft gospel of comfort, a social Marxist gospel that justifies theft to be redistributed for equity and sustainability's sake.

"They will certainly miss Jesus' return. They think themselves alive for their many activities yet have no change in their lives. They're lost, numbed in sins of pride, asleep and dreaming all is well. Turn back to Jesus!

"And then there are the Laodicean bridesmaids who are like lukewarm, tepid, filthy pond water. Yes, rich in the ways of man and in need of nothing. Justifying that the church must accept the world's norms and seeker-sensitive intellectual ways.

"They seek to escape judgment by redefining love as tolerance—anything goes. Getting prosperity from God is all this bunch is about! Their oil runs dry before they think themselves rich and in need of nothing.

"We've heard for years that there will be a big end-time outpouring, a great revival, an awakening. Yet ask anyone what the message of this end-time event is about, and they really can't tell you. But here in Revelation 2 and 3 is the very message of that great end-time revival—an awakening. However…"

As I listened to the message, I noticed many folks felt convicted as the healing waters began to wash the mud out of their eyes. Pastor Loos continued.

"In the years ahead, this infection will spread. Teaching will say that there is no need to pray—God knows it all. No need for spiritual warfare, no need for discipleship, especially no need to live right before God and man, and definitely no need to help change the diapers of those babes in Christ because that is all works-based and oh, how it smells!

"Ecumenicalism will arise with its 'conform the church to the world's culture mindset.' Occult works and new age signs and wonders will enter the church by the naïve masquerading as the true. Old Jezebel ruled behind the king to help set up her kingdom on earth—that will be heard again taking shape inside the church!

"The holiness of God will be forgotten by many. Not the 'holier than thou' kind of holiness, but rather 'be separate from the world system.' We have no part with the ways of Belial in any form. We need the Lord's holiness to separate us unto Himself.

"That is the holiness we need now, in this dark hour. Lord Jesus, let Your holiness arise! Let Your holiness arise in our hearts! Separate us—separate us unto You!

"We have a job, folks of God, we are a team. If we do not do our job as a team, folks, people get hurt. One has this spiritual gift, and another has that gift. Let's learn to blend and gel together, so our supply of oil never runs dry, so we don't slumber in all the bad doctrines that are sure plentiful in the dark days that lie ahead.

"People are hurting and in need of mending. Jesus is called the Great Physician, and we are predestined to be transformed into whose image (see Romans 8:29)? Now, whose image are you more concerned with—yours? Let the holiness of God arise! Let it arise! Let it arise!"

* * *

We had a lot of hands and feet at Holy Tabernacle. Believe it or not, we all flowed together well. We all ministered by the grace and power of God through the gifts of the Holy Spirit to each other and to those outside.

We all were *definitely* not perfect. No, not at all. What we had was Jesus cleaning the mud out of our eyes as we helped each other learn to walk alone to the pool of healing.

We learned to trust the Bible, and by that trust we discovered our flaws that needed healing. We accepted each other and bore each other's burdens. This is lacking today in so many assemblies. I guess many vessels of oil have run dry.

Despite our flaws, God's grace worked through us, bringing souls to Christ and helping them grow, find courage, and pass on what we learned. This came about through real Bible study. We prayed, sought the Lord, learned from each other and our mistakes, owned up to them, repented, and became responsible.

The older saints of God taught the younger folks. No one was segregated by age group or isolated from each other except the very young children who learned in Sunday school about Jesus.

Together we helped change spiritual diapers from time to time. In doing so, we learned the ways of the Lord and how the gifts of the Holy Spirit work as God wills, not as we will. In the process we found healing for our souls. *How about you?*

Sadly, it is not like that much these days. Something changed. Many pastors come across like Mr. Hip and Brother Cool, so seeker-sensitive they lose sight of the gospel of Christ. Instead, everything is a polished program. Unsaved musicians are hired to play in praise bands so everything sounds perfect. *What fellowship has light with darkness?* You have laser light shows, Broadway-style productions, then hear a short 20-minute sermonette about Jesus being the best servant you'll ever have to meet your every need. There is no condemnation, only lollipops and roses along with all the cookies and ice cream you can eat.

Much of the modern church world is now culturally relevant, a consumer market-driven church! The result is that many folks find themselves lost in a sea of people who do not know the inner pain of one another. You hear the same old claptrap about "if you do these steps you'll attain great prosperity." However, many grow broke instead. Envy is created among God's people.

Then there is the call for social justice portrayed in cute film clips shown above the pulpit stage to save the planet, stop climate change, pay reparations, redistribute the wealth, and for all to bow at the altar of pride.

The church has become no different from the Western educational system, grooming a lost generation of youth to be without a moral compass. We see the fruit of it now: high suicide rates, hopelessness, rise in crime, and worldwide chaos. The devil comes to steal, kill, and destroy by using cunning deceptions so folks deny the reality they see. This downward spiral occurs in any nation and any people who forget God.

What's the cure for the church? Do you think it needs a little dip in the pool?

Dear Lord Jesus, grant us all the ability to see through Your eyes of grace and endure what we see. Give us the courage to change, so we become a better reflection of You and of ourselves.

CHAPTER SEVEN

TWO HOURS BEFORE HEAVEN

"To do righteousness and justice is more acceptable to the Lord than sacrifice."

—Proverbs 21:3 NKJV

"This is ZWTW Radio, Tina Largo Crawford here, on Walk the Walk Christian Radio. Did Tom find God's life-altering grace to become the Lord's *poiema,* workmanship, mentioned in Ephesians 2:10, Bryan?"

"Yes, he sobered up. If I recall correctly, he became a medical professional working in a hospital. He became a devout Christian, got married, and raised a fine family in the faith.

"We learn to grow out of our old lifestyles, just as Ezekiel 36:26-27 reveals. Over time those truly saved will experience measurable change in their personal lives. The Holy Spirit guarantees such transformation."

Tina spoke up, "Strange how the little things we do for one person are all interconnected with other people whom we never know, and all put together by God. He changes a sinner into a saint—like the metamorphosis of a caterpillar into a butterfly. Just amazing!"

As the hosts chatted back and forth, my mind wandered back to the night before heaven happened.

* * *

After the sermon, 30 people came forward to be baptized. This made me duty-bound to the sound board and I got grumpier. *No sleep tonight.* The service finally ended after midnight. *Thank gawd,* I said to myself. *Oh, so agonizingly late.* There would be no sleep tonight. *Didn't we baptize enough already? Whoops! Sorry, Lord!*

Tom was quiet and very sober. Several parishioners invited him out to eat at a late-night diner, ensuring Tom would get home safely. That problem was solved. Then the band just up and left me holding the bag!

I was fuming, because I had no help putting everything away. Finally, I secured the building and locked all the doors. *How unfair! Poor pitiful me!*

I left church around two in the morning in a "sour caterpillar" mood and drove 40 minutes to the outskirts of town to reach home.

Oncoming headlights flashed into my eyes; my mind raced: *What will the pastor think of me bringing Tom? Friends left tonight without helping to put all the equipment away. Is this church stuff really worth this? Dang, I'll never get any sleep tonight!* Now I was complaining. All I could think about was getting up at 5 a.m. and rushing off to work. *Was church worth it—all that work for such ungrateful folk?*

Hmm, who is really ungrateful here?
Have you ever felt that way?

Oh my, will I lose my salvation if I don't keep doing sacrificial things for God? I do not want to go back to that awful place. Is this my lot? That question rocked my world after my death experience several years before when I literally experienced an awful place. By God's grace alone, and only by that, I was allowed to return— so undeserved, *so undeserved.* This weighed heavily on me. I did not deserve to return to this mortal life. I felt guilty, ashamed.

Oncoming headlights from a passing truck triggered another episode. I began to sweat and tremble because the memories were still vivid and real. *Please, God, I never want to go back to that awful place!* Oh, how the memories haunted me.

* * *

I followed a foul creature into the vilest of recesses of the pit of hell. Down we went into a foul-smelling fountain in the midst of a large vat of goo-like black tar that poured forth out of earth's bowels inside a strange building.

We walked endlessly on the hot, dry, dusty mire in this pit. Flames rose here and there. The heat was so hot that at times I felt as though my eyes were roasting. We passed myriads of people trapped in cubes, cells, chambers of living death, having the true "them" uncovered and exposed—reaping what they had sown.

White, moth-like creatures fluttered about. Grotesque serpentine creatures stoked the prisoners with graphic remembrances of former lives. All who were trapped here willingly chose their life direction, ignoring God's call for rescue, and I could hear the echoes of wretched laughter.

I passed soul after soul trapped all alone in their own personal fissures. Worms and wicked moths with teeth crawled about. Each soul here was realizing who and what they were really like made manifest. Each was sealed forever in this banished doom.

Post-traumatic stress is real.

* * *

"This is Night Ryder here on ZWTW Christian Radio, walk the walk and talk the talk, glad to have our guest here. So, B.W, what happened next?"

CHAPTER EIGHT

SECONDS BEFORE HEAVEN

"Why me, Lord? A once cantankerous Christian who used to lack such faith in Your ways—"

My rented trailer, *home*, appeared in the headlights. My dog was glad to see me. It was a little before 3 a.m., and I was exhausted. *If I could just rest a bit, I could drag myself to work within two hours.*

Instead, my mind raced with anger to justify my self-pity at staying late at church, putting away sound equipment, and cleaning up while everyone bailed. *Yes, church would be great if it weren't for all the people.* If anyone would have wanted another favor, I imagined punching them right in the nose. *Who cares! Why am I doing all these churchy things? For what? The ungrateful louts!*

My mind changed gears. *There are people out there who are sending themselves to hell. Some will make it to heaven, some will not. No one will believe me—I've seen hell.* What right did I have complaining about being inconvenienced? After all, were not souls saved tonight?

I must work harder to do good enough, or else—hell, if I screw up. What's the use? I was tired. There would be no sleep tonight. I would just rest with my eyes closed till the rays of the dawning sun shone through the east bedroom window. That is, if my alarm clock failed.

My German shepherd jumped up on the bed and curled up by my feet. *Dogs—all heart, and some days a little short on brains, but other times they're smarter than we are!*

My mind raced while lying in bed. I had trained myself to lie still with closed eyes to rest. It was something I learned to do while on a 21-day outward-bound mountaineering survival skills course that I took back in 1977, which trained me to keep going in survival situations with little sleep.

Suddenly, a booming voice shook the room:

ARISE! AWAKE! ARISE! STAND TO YOUR FEET!

Light, brighter than the noonday sun, flooded my room. My dog's collar jingled as she lifted her head at the voice. *Am I dreaming?*

Without thinking, I yelled out, "Shut up! I need sleep—I'm tired! Go away!" I tossed the covers up over my head. Brilliant light blazed through the sheets. Was this the early morning sun? When I tossed the blankets off, there was no light. It was still night.

"Man, that was weird," I mused. "It's 3:15 in the morning. Man, I need rest…"

Without warning, the voice bellowed loudly.

ARISE! AWAKE! ARISE! STAND TO YOUR FEET!

The room lit up. This time my dog bounded up, shaking the bed. What did I do? Pulled the covers back over my head, yelling out, "Not now! I am too tired!"

I wasn't in a holy mood, nor was I seeking what was about to happen. Opening my eyes, the room was dark. My dog was happily yipping like she was greeting some well-known friend. I got up to let the dog outside, but she would not move off the bed. She seemed to be looking at something standing in the hallway, though nothing was there.

Climbing back in bed, I closed my eyes. Grumpy is an understatement. *Tom, the church, and now my lovable dumb dog. I never get any sleep.*

Living out in the countryside is quiet, and the dark stillness of the night lulled me again into thinking, *Some dream.*

A brilliant light engulfed the room. The voice bellowed a third time:

ARISE! AWAKE! ARISE! STAND TO YOUR FEET!

Pulling the covers over my head again, I shouted out, "*NOT NOW, it's too early!* Go away…what?"

The intense light abruptly went out. My dog jumped off the bed. I pitched the sheets off my head and sat straight up. *Oh my God, I missed the rapture!*

As I bounded out of the bed, I saw my dog happily yipping, looking up, and wagging her tail. Her ears were going up and down like someone was petting her. I sensed a great presence. Intense peace and compassion filled the room. Then a still, quiet voice spoke deep within my soul:

Do you remember how you left before?

"Yes…"

Do you remember how you left before?

"Yes," I said as I lay back down. As soon as my head hit the pillow, I felt myself being lifted up right out of my body, as though I had died, even though I had not.

I passed through a large, empty storage cabinet located above my bed, knocking the door off its tracks. After I returned, that door was lying on the cabinet floor. There is no way it could have come off its track all by itself.

This was no dream. It was a visitation from the Lord Himself to calm me down about seeing the pit of hell a few years before. Seeing such a place pressed in on me in ways hard to explain. Why? One cannot talk about such an experience without fear of being hauled away and ridiculed.

I had PTSD even though I didn't realize it at the time. I had nightmares; and sights and sounds, even certain odors, triggered memories, taking me back to a land of leering eyes. Heat. Malice. Strange beings rubbing their hands with glee. Others waiting to pounce. A cacophony of vile wickedness and revenge, waiting to tear me to shreds at one wrong word. How could I report any of this in the midst of a scoffing world?

With that, let me say I am not Paul the apostle, nor do I claim to be, but I can relate to what Paul wrote: "whether in the body or out of the body, I do not know." Heaven.

I received no new revelation, no mandate, no call from it. The only thing I retained is what is found in the Bible, along with an understanding that I lacked before about how the Bible points to Jesus Christ, our blessed Savior forever—amen.

In and for Him alone all glory must shine, and none for me. Can I get a witness?

CHAPTER NINE

HEAVEN NEARS!

"The Lord reigns...Clouds and darkness surround Him; righteousness and justice are the foundation of His throne."
—Psalm 97:1-2 NKJV

"What was it like? What happened next?" questioned Night Ryder.

I found myself floating in the same pleasant darkness toward the same intense, profound, brilliant light that I saw once before when I faced judgment. However, this time an extreme sense of great joy, peace, and acceptance engulfed me.

Best I can explain it—it was like going home where an embrace of love awaits after a long, painful ordeal. No more sorrows, tears, pain, or sin.

I was going home, a real eternal home belonging to God's house. No words can capture what it was like. There I was drifting effortlessly toward the brilliant radiance of the Lord of glory as His adopted child, an enemy no more, fully accepted by what Christ alone has done. Ephesians describes it like this:

> *Blessed be the God and Father of our Lord Jesus Christ, who has blessed us with every spiritual blessing in the heavenly places in Christ, just as He chose us in Him*

before the foundation of the world, that we should be holy and without blame before Him in love, having predestined us to adoption as sons by Jesus Christ to Himself, according to the good pleasure of His will, to the praise of the glory of His grace, by which He made us accepted in the Beloved (Ephesians 1:3-6 NKJV).

All this is so undeserved. It is only because of what He has done that makes us *accepted in the beloved.* I felt those words in the deepest and fullest sense. These are healing words to a wounded soul with a hurting heart. Rejection and fear are arrested, gone.

This begins in this life when we become born again and becomes actualized in the life to come as we approach heaven. For now, God has a purpose for our lives in which the hurts in life are healed so we can comfort the hurting with the same comfort that we have been comforted, set free, by God.

Blessed be the God and Father of our Lord Jesus Christ, the Father of mercies and God of all comfort, who comforts us in all our tribulation, that we may be able to comfort those who are in any trouble, with the comfort with which we ourselves are comforted by God (2 Corinthians 1:3-4 NKJV).

I worry here as I do not want to be misunderstood. Life can be harsh. Please do not take what I am sharing here as an excuse to check out or end your life. Read and re-read that verse. We go through things so that we can help others in ways no one else can. Jesus will get you through.

Here in this mortal life, we learn that we can trust in God's faithfulness that upholds us and gets us through whatever comes our way in life—the good, the bad, and the ugly. He is a faithful God and unchanging in that faithfulness. He calls us His beloved. He restores, adopts, and reconciles us, and by His Holy Spirit and by His word we learn how to live. We learn what it means to have a heavenly Father. The fellowship that was stolen in this life is restored.

What I share is emotional for me. The feeling of going home as accepted in Him is truly profound and life-altering. No matter how many times we bumble and stumble in this life, remember that as Christians we are *accepted in the beloved!*

Floating toward the light of God's glory, I was embraced by the faithfulness of God. That embrace has not left me. This embrace grants you insight into the sovereignty of God that is difficult to adequately describe. I will share more on this later.

I was being pulled by an irresistible tide. Heavenly music resounded from innumerable unknown instruments declaring life, all about the one and only true living God! I was going home!

Amidst this heavenly cacophony, multiplied millions of voices in one vast choir sang in the language of heaven, proclaiming the full glory of God with intimate knowledge and understanding and wisdom, revealing Almighty God and His splendor. I was going home, accepted in the beloved!

I was approaching the same huge rock suspended in darkness I saw once before. Behind the rock, it was like a curtain lifted, exposing a glorious land behind a high wall. Jesus paved the land of heaven behind the rock with His own blood, for His beloved—me! Going home!

The light of God's glory consumed me as it was emitted from Jesus, who stood upon the rock suspended betwixt heaven and earth and hell. I was bathed in a brilliant cleansing tide.

I was going home! Oh, what a feeling! Home! Accepted in the beloved. *I ask, are you?*

* * *

Tina could not help herself: "Whoa, accepted in the beloved—that's deep! Praise You, Jesus—we are accepted in the beloved, for by His grace alone we stand. GLORY! GLORY! GLORY!"

"Wow," Night Ryder said excitedly. "The dark void—that darkness you traversed reminds me of this verse in the Bible in Exodus 20:21, when Moses drew near thick darkness where God was.

"Exodus 20:20 (KJV) explains the reason why this is: *'And Moses said unto the people, Fear not: for God is come to prove you, and that his fear may be before your faces, that ye sin not.'*"

"Well, I'm not Moses by a long shot," I replied to Ryder, laughing a little. "First John 1:5 states that in Him there is no darkness. Yet in Psalm 97:1-2 (NKJV), it says: *'The Lord reigns… Clouds and darkness surround Him; righteousness and justice are the foundation of His throne.'*"

"And again, like you said, God hid Himself in thick darkness on Mount Sinai, as verse 20 says, to *prove*—test—see what was inside the people back then and for us today too."

Tina interjected, "That sounds like there are two types of darkness. One represents evil, ignorance, and spiritual blindness. And the other, God hides behind to reveal something about *ourselves*, so we learn who He is—that He is trustworthy. As you said, B.W., so we learn to trust in His faithfulness. What do you think?"

I responded, "There are several meanings why God hides behind clouds of darkness. First off, darkness reveals the nature of sin and that we need a savior. Darkness helps us to rely on the Lord's help to combat sin in our lives. We never will be perfectly sinless in this life. But we can learn to be free from one sin at a time, so we sin less than the day before and finally will be without sin when we arrive in heaven.

"Also, the darkness the Lord hides behind helps develop a healthy respect, fear of the Lord, so people learn to mature and stop toying with God, His promises, His word, gifts, and ways as mere playthings, as some sort of ego booster and all that. Here we learn what it means that *'righteousness and justice are the foundation of His throne.'*

"We live in a dark world where evil is revealed, sin specified, iniquity proved, and rebellion defined. We need a saving from what is inside us. Sadly, most rely on other things, like self, ideas, or even the devil, as saviors to improve their lot in life. Darkness reveals that which one has the most faith in.

"God sends His light into darkness. His light obviates the darkness in us. Just as Jesus said in John 3 about people loving darkness more than His light. Why?"

Ryder answered, "They love their own ways. You can rightly say darkness seen in this mortal life is used to cause people to sicken of it so they turn back to the Lord, because they see the truth—only He can save and no other."

"That's right," I said. "Jesus came as the light of the world. The gospel of the light of Christ opens the eyes so people can recognize the truth and become saved, or they harden their heart harder because they love darkness more.

"In all of this, God proves Himself absolutely, just way beyond what our human pea brains can think of. No one can say, 'God, You predestined me to hell.' Actually, you sent yourself there. Why? Because you love darkness, and you trust in another type of savior who can't save and does not have more to offer than the light Christ Jesus brings."

"This makes me think of the subject of God's predestination," piped Night Ryder. "Some camps say God just arbitrarily selects who is saved and who is not based solely on sovereign whim. Others say God allows free moral will or allows by His permissive will. There is so much confusion on this. Any insights?"

I responded, "Well, that opens a can of worms. I am not sure I can do justice here trying to describe God's sovereign nature that I experienced in heaven. All I can do is try."

* * *

God is not a divine puppet master causing you to scratch your nose or sending the molester to molest. God's sovereignty is greater than that. Yes, it is true that God does not need to further consider if any man should come before Him in judgment (see Job 34:23). This is because God knows what we all are like before we were born. He also knows what we'll be like without any divine intervention if we are allowed to continue in our fallen state.

God lives true to His own standards of His divine character traits with no shadow of turning. He is the faithful God!

God's sovereignty is based on His own all-powerful foreknowledge tempered and guided by all that He says. He always proves Himself true to His own character traits and nature without any contradiction.

For example, Isaiah 1:18 clearly states God's desire to reason with us. Elsewhere, it states to choose whom we will serve (see Joshua 24:15; Deuteronomy 30:19). This is consistent with God's absolute sense of justice. After all, He is a God of justice.

Denying this would prove God unjust, by exercising arbitrary whim to select a certain number of folks for the abyss without reason. That would be contrary to God's character traits found in the Bible—a just God who said, "Come, let us reason together." God gives us free moral will. Despite the fact that God knows the final outcome, He still allows people to choose whom they will serve anyway. Truly, God is just in all His ways.

By such foreknowing, out of those who reject Him, like Pharaoh, He uses them and does with them whatever He wills, without any injustice involved. God knew Pharaoh would reject Him and go back on his word. Pharaoh's heart was hardened already before he tried to cross the sea. With that, God's glory and power was shown as He rescued His people.

Don't get me wrong, God can make things happen when needed, but He does so without any violation to His character or nature. God gives us the freedom of will so we can choose to obey Him or not. No one can say to the Lord, "You never gave me an honest chance because You damned me before I was ever born." How so? Answer: His word creates choice. His word cuts to the heart, revealing the thoughts and intentions of the human heart. One can either come to his or her senses or reject Him completely (Romans 1:20; Joshua 24:14-15).

The nature of His word justly grants choice. Before we were saved, we never realized there was a such a choice. We went about life, lost. The lines between right and wrong blurred. Blind to our own need for a savior. The word of God reveals the heart. A choice granted when before we had none.

CHAPTER TEN

THE CRIMSON WAY

"This was the appearance of the likeness of the glory of the Lord. So when I saw it, I fell on my face, and I heard a voice of One speaking."

—Ezekiel 1:28 NKJV

A great wall of brilliant light came into view as I approached. Heaven beckons beyond.

There was Jesus. Dazzling beams of the most beautiful light came from Him standing upon the rock near what I thought to be the sheep gate mentioned in John 10:7-9. Past the gate meandered a beautiful pathway of uncut stones stretching alongside this grand wall. Each was perfectly placed and studded with majestic uncut gems emitting a filtered light. Off in the near distance, I saw a huge white pearl interlaced with living, heavenly blue streaks moving within it. In it was a gate, an entranceway.

The dazzling light from Jesus consumed me. Before I knew it, I landed gently before the Lord of glory. My eyes adjusted to the light as I fell to the ground before Him. A loving welcome reverberated through my entire soul bringing healing and awe to my wounded heart.

During my prior after-death experience, I had done the same—I fell before the Lord undone, fully exposed as a sinner who abused and manipulated the love of God and others. But this time was different. I was fully alive and accepted by Him at the same time. I was cured of my pride—it was knocked out of me.

Though not sure how it happened, I found myself standing before Him gazing into His eyes—the Lord Jesus Christ, God who came in the flesh. Who destroyed all the works of the devil! There He stood, the living word of God. The one whom John wrote about in the first chapter of his gospel account, literally the second person of the divine Trinity, the living Word (*Logos*). When the living God speaks, His word lives to carry it out. This time He was not wearing a hood of judgment as he did a few short years back. His whole being beamed with shades of astounding light. This was a joyous homecoming. Our Christian journey in this life readies us to behold His glory, my friends!

People always ask, "What did Jesus look like? Are you sure you saw Him? Why do people who claim to have seen Him describe Him differently from each other?"

My answer is a question: How can you really explain what Jesus looks like?

He first appeared to me as very Jewish. He had almond-shaped eyes, and what eyes they were! At first, they appeared to be hazel—almost the same color as mine but with a bit more brown. He had olive skin—very Jewish in appearance.

His eyes seemed to radiate a light within that would change the color of His pupils, appearing blue, brown, or hazel depending on the intensity of the light. What eyes! I was mesmerized. I felt acceptance beyond what words can express, and I was humbled.

I found myself standing before the Author of eternity. Counselor. Wonderful. Prince of Peace, Soundness, Wholeness.

Almighty God. Son of Man—all reflected in His eyes toward me and into the depths of my soul with compassion and love profound.

What did He look like? During the time I was with Him, one moment He appeared as the Lord of glory similar to the description in Revelation 19, then very human and Jewish. Next, His appearance changed to resurrected Lord. He appeared as the one called the Son of Man written about in Ezekiel 1:16, Daniel 7:13-28, and Matthew 13:41. Why did He appear differently?

His appearance changes. An example of this is found in Revelation 19 appearing as a mighty warrior. Another is found in Mark 16:12-13 appearing in another form to the two disciples traveling along the road. Peter and John didn't recognize Him along the shore of the Galilee in John 21:1-14. Now I understand why.

Jesus appeared most often like a strong, weathered Jewish man, rather than resurrected and in a glorified form. He looks like the Son of Man, the Ancient of Days who entered our world so we could become His children, be reconciled and adopted into the household of God and healed of our wounds. Home!

You could not mistake His eyes though. Windows of the soul where you gazed into the depth of God's love and justice in a manner indescribably felt and known, yet incredibly hard to adequately describe.

I met His gaze, and I was embraced by the warmth that had been robbed from me in life. His gaze restored me, reconciled me. "Welcome!" Jesus spoke. "Welcome!"

Do you hear that? Welcome! Oh my, I am undone by that welcome even today.

He forgave me. All was forgiven! I was welcomed!

He spoke with words of life that fill your thoughts with complete understanding. Then He smiled and I was filled with joy! He spoke to me in a way that was clearer than ever before. I had heard Him by means of thought before while facing judgment after I died. This time, He spoke words out loud—words that had layers of meaning and that unfolded within me. Suddenly, I had a warehouse full of knowledge, wisdom, and understanding unpacked all at once.

I wondered how people could betray Jesus, mock Him, put Him on trial, then crucify Him who healed and set people free. He who has seen Jesus has seen the Father—seen His heart, as Jesus said to Philip.

Yet at one point I did not trust Jesus, and now I was forgiven and standing before Him—accepted! Yes, I was standing accepted before the one who exposed my own iniquity in my heart, who forgave me. That began the healing and cleansing of my soul.

"Welcome. You have seen a lot." He smiled and beckoned me, "Come." Jesus motioned to what I later came to call the "crimson way." It was a pathway that meandered up to a gate seen in the near distance. "Let's go for little walk. Be troubled no more. You've seen a lot—peace. Come."

All I could do was look around and pay attention to everything. Jesus would from time to time ask me what I saw and have me glance at things a bit.

Looking down at the crimson trail made of tiny, reddish-brown, uncut stones, I was amazed by a beautiful hedge that followed it. Interspaced alongside the edges of the trail there were crimson rocks clustered together.

Birds chirped as though resounding God's glory. Why? I guess God likes birds and can do what He wants, right? God is not beholden to our theological arguments on such matters. Some folks get mad if you say there are animals in heaven. God is sovereign and He if wants animals in heaven, why not? He can, and who are we to say He can't? Think about it. Jesus comes back riding a white horse, right?

This macadamized way felt soothing to the feet. I came to the edge of the hedge. Beautiful flowers and well-groomed plants and trees lined the lane. The smell of heaven permeated, dispensing wisdom, understanding, knowledge of the holiness and harmony that filled His house (Proverbs 24:3-4).

I was moving toward the perfection of God by which He reconciled all things to Himself just as Colossians 1:19-23 says.

He spoke to me, smiling. "What do you see along the way?"

"I think that in this mortal life," I replied, "we Christians just begin to walk our own personal crimson way paved by the blood of Your cross, Jesus, so we are no longer Your foes. As we walk, we find cleansing for our entry into heaven,"

Heaven is home! Finally, in heaven, we are home!

Oh, how blessed are the feet of those who bear the gospel of peace (see Romans 10:15).

Teach me Your way, O Lord; I will walk in Your truth; unite my heart to fear Your name (Psalm 86:11 NKJV).

CHAPTER ELEVEN

AT THE GATE

"This is the gate of the Lord, through which the righteous shall enter."

—Psalm 118:20 NKJV

The Trinity of God is a mystery. Jesus, the Lord of glory, walked close beside and slightly ahead of me. Like I say often, no one can explain the orthodox doctrine of the Trinity, the triune nature of the Godhead, very well.

The Bible says God is unique, that there is none like Him (see Isaiah 46:9; 45:21). Therefore, His three-in-one triune form of oneness is unlike anything we know. God is Spirit but do we know what His divine spiritual essence looks like? No one does!

God's nature is revealed in His word through Jesus (see John 8:42; 16:27-28). The apostle John mentions that Jesus is the Logos, the living Word of God in John 1:1-14. The living Word who proceeds forth from the Father and declares His will and purposes.

The Father, Son, and Holy Ghost are of the same divine essence. This is how God rolls. God is the living God. Jesus told Phillip, "He who has seen Me has seen God."

The Father speaks, and Jesus carries out the Father's will. At both Jesus' baptism and transfiguration, the Father spoke that

Jesus was His beloved Son whom He is well pleased. Jesus went about doing good, casting out devils and healing many, and His Father was pleased. Jesus chased out the money changers and confronted the sins of the religious hierarchy, and His Father was pleased. Jesus wept in the garden and carried out the will of His Father, who sent Him to the cross, and who was pleased.

Likewise, the Holy Spirit proceeds from the Father to sanctify, to prepare the way, to display the might of the Lord, and to establish and seal a matter.

The Holy Spirit is God's Spirit. I heard a minister once say that both Jesus and the Holy Spirit are the living arms of the Lord, one with the Father, co-eternal and co-equal with the Him. The Bible reveals that there is none like God. His oneness of being is unlike any human concept of oneness. We cannot make Him fit our ideas. Moses desired to see God in His full form but was warned by God that he could not live if he did. The Lord God hid Moses in a cleft of a rock as He passed by; thus, God reveals Himself to humanity in theophanies. He is a God of truth.

Some folks like to describe God's triune nature as water, vapor, and ice. Others illustrate the nature of an orange. The juice represents the Father, the fruit/seed is Jesus, and the peel is the Holy Spirit who establishes and makes whole. All illustrations like this fall short. I suggest you study your Bible and the words of Jesus on this matter.

In Isaiah 48:16-17, God spoke in the third person. Jesus was known in the Old Testament as the Malak (messenger, word bearer, task doer) of YHWH. He appeared before Manoah and others.

This is He who walked with me in heaven, my kinsman redeemer. I cannot describe adequately how awed I was. I was with the Lord of glory who came in the likeness of men to redeem lost humanity back to Himself. He is the living expression of God's love, kindness, grace, mercy, justice, holiness, righteousness, truth. All that the Father is, He expresses.

Yet He walked with me, one so greatly undeserving of such an honor. You can say I was undone again, this time in a good manner. Sometimes I weep, thinking about this.

We walked along this beautifully adorned trail as it followed alongside this grand wall made of uncut rock and gemstones that literally beamed forth the knowledge of the Holy One. The beauty seemed to reveal that God's goodness was shining forth. He is good to all, just in all His ways, and completely righteous, separate, grand, and holy above all others. Sovereign!

Great is that mystery. He, Jesus, the living Word of God, came in the likeness of man but never surrendered His divinity—He remained 100 percent God and 100 percent man during His time on earth.

He refrained from using His full authority and came as a servant to set the record straight. On earth, He knew the heart of everyone around Him and beyond. He voluntarily refrained from exercising His full divinity as Philippians 2:1-11 says.

He who sees Him sees the Father, Jesus told Phillip. John 3:16 begins with, "For God so loved." Think about it. That is who I walked with, then and now. How about you?

* * *

Suddenly, Tina's voice came through my headset, "The Bible mentions the heavenly temple area in Ezekiel 40:5 and the New Jerusalem in Revelation 21 having walls. It seems no one quite understands why there would be such walls in heaven."

"Yes, I find that Bible commentators largely speculate on such walls," Night Ryder responded. "Any insights you have on it, Bryan?"

"I agree, no one fully knows the whys of these types of walls, but after seeing a wall there, I can only offer my opinion on why. So, I ask folks to search out this matter your own. With that, here is my take on it."

* * *

Whatever their purpose, one thing is sure: the current heavenly city has a wall. This seems to be alluded to in Psalm 48:1-2. However, hell is different, pit-like. Broad is the way to destruction.

To me, heaven has an immigration policy—no one can enter unless by the crimson, that narrow way. Therefore, one enters by faith in God's grace revealed by the cross of Christ. That's the only way to become a citizen of heaven. By this the wheat is separated from the chaff.

Our trust in His awesome faithfulness was broken by the fall of man. That confidence in God's faithfulness was restored by Jesus Christ's death on the cross, which proves God's mercy, goodness, and forgiveness is true. "God so loved." Faith is restored when you look upon the cross and see that God's beloved Son died there, revealing man's desperately twisted heart that tried to justify all his ways.

Why this wall? Maybe the purpose of the heavenly wall I saw is to protect creation from the full manifest glory of God's united essence. With that, I'll let people speculate.

Perhaps the wall's purpose is comparable to Moses not being able to look on God's full glory (Exodus 33:17-23). God truly knows our frame; we are but dusty clay. Jesus' crimson way purifies us as we travel its path of mortal life preparing us to enter the fullness of the glory of God's holiness that resides behind the wall and which seemed to me to be filtering through the wall, revealing what Psalm 19:1 (NKJV) conveys: *"The heavens declare the glory of God; and the firmament shows His handiwork."*

I recall being so vividly astounded by the wall and its gates, so much so my mind could not comprehend all the why's? Maybe I was allowed to see in some way what Ezekiel saw in Ezekiel 40:5-16? Again, I do not know because so much of what I saw in Heaven is indescribable, overwhelming.

The grandest gate ever seen loomed ahead. What a gate! It was made of one huge white pearl with pure heavenly blue streaks reflecting within it. This blue was only known to heaven. Its white reminded me of the ultimate purity, and only those who have been made pure by the blood of the Lamb enter heaven here. Around it stood angelic beings. Others were emerging from its long corridor either entering or exiting the gate. In the Bible, gates were the area where people would gather to hear news or proclamations. At the gates, justice was carried out. From the gates, people were sent forth to perform tasks and gather provisions for their assignments.

I stood with the Lord upon a slight rise, gazing at this amazing scene. Heavenly messengers came and went to perform tasks and assignments, all sealed by God's word somewhere deep inside of heaven's land. I watched how the angelic were sent forth to provide courage, restore wavering faith, do battle against the forces of darkness, and help with provision. They also help folks make connections with people and events as well as delay people so they avoid harmful accidents, in some cases saving folks during a disaster.

Some were escorting a saint, who entered eternity nanoseconds before, to the place behind the wall. I also saw living creatures going forth from the gate to do many various assignments and tasks God decreed upon the earth.

Others were sent forth for spiritual warfare in the way Daniel 10:13 describes—to do battle and bring messages of answered prayer to God's people. If you saw some of these, you would be terrified of them. They were strange, majestic beings. Some were all eyes amidst what appeared like wheels. Ezekiel saw the same. How can you explain angelic beings who moved about in any direction, yet their faces were always toward the throne of God?

Others had four faces on various types of bodies. Many had bronzed skin and some appeared human-like but were not. Some rode on disks of light and wheels, while others had wings of light rather than feathers. There were those who had no wings but just flew carrying out God's will. There were flaming creatures like serpents. Some of these had arms and four feet. Seraphim appeared as ribbons of flaming light and sent messages and proclamations of God's justice and praise.

Others investigated the ways of salvation and helped turn God's true ministers into flames of God's fire. I suggest reading 1 Peter 1:12 and Hebrew 1:7 for the details on this.

Some were protecting; some were bearing messages. For example, a preacher somewhere on earth was granted a sermon to present to the flock. Messages were whispered into obedient ears. Anointing and gifts were granted to those whom the Lord trusts. A vast many watched over humanity and the universe to do God's will.

These are all God's servants, His holy, loyal angels, who will never allow you to glorify them or worship them, but with silent frequency carry out the Lord's will revealed from His heavenly council room.

It is true, God is capable of doing all things by Himself. He needs no one, yet He chooses to work through His faithful ones. He enjoys those He created and includes them in His decisions and plans just as 1 Kings 22:19-28 illustrates.

He is the faithful and true living God, *absolutely* all-powerful!

The crimson way, in this mortal life, prepares us to behold His glory that awaits beyond this entrance, and this was only one of twelve gates. I stood there amazed at how jubilant yet reverent the angels were about performing their tasks. Then the Lord of glory smiled and nodded, "See."

Standing there by the crimson gate, I began gaining an intense respect for Jesus as the Lord of glory, righteous, holy, and true as well as my closest and dearest friend. There was Jesus before me beaming with power, compassion, life—what else can I say? We entered the gate.

* * *

His gifts, purposes, and callings are not playthings to amuse us, nor are they for putting on a show to make people all balloon-brained, filled with thoughts lofty as helium. Lifting oneself up as someone so grand, special, above the commoners.

The acclaim of men and women is fleeting. The smile from the Lord is enduring. As He watches us here on earth during our walk on our own personal crimson way, is it His smile or your personal acclaim you seek?

Folks, Jesus shows us the Father in the written gospel accounts. We have His word on that. Stay true to the Bible. Avoid chasing after some new thing and ever newer revelations that draw you away from the Bible. Why?

You will stray. If you do, know this: His chastening proves His love true. Return to the Lord, my friend, return!

The enemy indeed appears as angels of light granting new revelations and new ways to keep you away from God's word recorded in the book.

By His word, the Bible, we are warned, develop discernment, learn just who God is and how to hear Him, follow Him, trust Him, obey Him with love in the heart. We learn that His love has boundaries. What He says is right and wrong, not what we or culture determines.

So, if you respect God, become a student of the Bible; devour every word. Remember, in the Bible Jesus revealed the Father's heart to lost humanity. He did good, healed, showed mercy, endured tribulations, and was the best teacher.

He forgave, He rebuked, He convicted the ungodly and divided light from darkness during creation. He did good things, and for them He was nailed to the cross. That is what some people do with goodness—mistreat it. Think about it.

CHAPTER TWELVE

THE CALVARY WAY

"Behold, the hour is at hand, and the Son of man is betrayed into the hands of sinners."

—Matthew 26:45 KJV

We entered the great pearly gate. Its beauty is beyond human description. Narrow is the way.

In heaven, everything has meaning. Even details convey profound truth. What you see unpacks things into your soul, explains things, causes you to seek out answers, ask questions, and learn how great God is in all He does.

In this life, the function of a pearl is for the protection against irritants that sneak into a mollusk's soft tissue. A mollusk encases the pollutant with layers of shell material till it is no longer a stressful irritant. Thus, it is changed into something beautiful, rare, invaluable, priceless, irreplaceable, no longer causing pain. So, God shapes us by the stress of life, sanctifying us so we are no longer dangerous, irritating pollutants. God's love does that—chastens, refines, making us a new creation in Christ.

To me, that is what this giant pearly gate represented. We all reach it by walking our own personal crimson way, sealed as His own. Heaven beckons beyond the door to those He purifies, no longer stressful irritants.

We entered its narrow corridor and beheld a unique, inexplicable sight.

This great pearl reflected its own light from within. Its white is a white that the human eye here on earth cannot see. Its blue swirls gently and slowly turned and moved about. Within the corridor, these emitted the gentlest, most extraordinary, beautiful bluish-purple light. Again, there are no colors on earth to rightly compare.

Jesus walked the narrow walkway before me, leading the way. He didn't speak to me, but I felt His words. As I began to rub my hand along the corridor wall, I was in wonder. It was rough, as though chiseled by four nails and a spear. Then it began.

* * *

Adjusting my headset, I asked, "Isaiah 53:6 says that the Lord placed on Jesus the iniquity of us all. How is this possible if He can't behold evil, as Habakkuk 1:13 mentions, and has no part in it as 2 Corinthians 6:14-15 says?

"That's deep," Night Ryder responded. "My guess, as learned in Bible college, would be that He did so through the law."

Tina interjected, "Yes, the law of sacrifice laid out in Leviticus explains how the high priest and people would lay their hands on the sacrifice, confessing their sins over it. Then, at Passover time, the high priest, as proxy, would lay his hands on the sacrifice to impute the sin of the people to the sacrificial lamb by means of declaring the sins of all upon it."

Ryder spoke up, "Even the high priest had to do likewise with another sacrifice for his own sins before the Passover lamb was slain as proxy for the people's sins. So the answer would be that through the law, God imputed the sin of all humanity through human agents" (see Isaiah 53; Romans 7; Galatians 3:24).

Tina responded, "Yes, on the night Jesus was betrayed, as stated in Mark 14:4, He was being handed over to sinners, thus fulfilling all the law's demands."

"Yep, Jesus fulfilled the law to a tee!" I chimed in. "Yes, to a tee."

"And in doing so, He revealed the iniquity hidden within the human heart that we do not even realize we have, just as Jeremiah 17:9-10 says. That's one heavy-duty object lesson!" Ryder said.

"Yes it is, yes it is. The 24 hours before the cross revealed the heart of humanity so that we may know it and stop justifying it, and so by His stripes we can be healed from it."

"What happened next?" asked Tina.

* * *

The corridor was narrow. Jesus walked ahead of me. Though He didn't speak to me directly, I felt His words. I touched the chiseled walls and bathed in the gentle, pure, bluish white emitted by this great pearl.

Rubbing my fingers along its hewn walls, I began to perceive the past in a cloudy manner while watching Jesus walk ahead of me along this narrow way. I cannot say what I saw was a vision.

I saw them plotting and scheming how to rid the world of Jesus. It was as though I was seeing into their hearts and their reasoning.

They thought Jesus was the one the prophet Daniel warned about who came to change seasons, times, and the law, such as the Sabbath law (see Daniel 7:25; Matthew 10:12). One who would declare Himself God (see Daniel 11:36). They really believed they were protecting the law that profited them beyond belief (see Matthew 23:23-25).

But they could not see Him as the suffering servant mentioned in Isaiah 53, sent to deal with sin and bring forth the New Covenant (see Jeremiah 31:31-33). I could hear them reason that if Jesus was really the Messiah, He would first come as a mighty king, throwing off Roman tyranny, so they could rule alongside Him, taking in the tithes and offerings of the world based on what Isaiah 60:5-11 and Isaiah 61:6-11 mentioned.

My, how they plotted, schemed, and altered the law to do as they pleased with Jesus. Then Judas came, playing both sides, right into their hands; and for 30 pieces of silver, Jesus, the Living Word, was betrayed.

I'm truly not sure how to explain it, but it was like being allowed to peer into the past from a short distance, as through a protective lens, as my fingers rubbed the wall.

What I saw was Calvary's way and how the events during the 24 hours before Jesus died on the cross revealed the factual condition of the human heart. We are all blind, too, and don't want to see or be reminded of it. Walking through this corridor revealed this to me as plain as day.

Though we might not like to acknowledge it, we need to ask ourselves, *How have we all betrayed, abandoned, mocked, rejected, scorned, neglected, or put on trial in our minds strangers, friends, family, ourselves, and God?*

> *The heart is deceitful above all things, and desperately wicked; who can know it?* (Jeremiah 17:9 NKJV)

How many times have we all passed the buck, told lies, or blamed another just to get ahead? The scriptures are true: "*All have sinned and fall short of the glory of God*" (Romans 3:23).

The events of those 24 hours leading to the crucifixion illustrate this. So we can say as Jeremiah wrote, "*Heal me, O Lord, and I shall be healed; save me, and I shall be saved*" (Jeremiah 17:14 NKJV).

All is evidenced by how we live right now—in our words, actions, and deeds. Will you but reach out your hand and confess these over the sacrificed Lamb?

Ahead of me Jesus walked, the One who paved the way chiseled by nails and the tip of a spear. My nails, my spear, and He forgave me.

Experiencing this left an impression on me. What kind of love would move someone to come and do this, show what we are like to each other, then pay our death penalty by bearing the wrath of God in our place for what we have done?

John 3:16 (NKJV) makes me weep to this day. "*For God so loved the world that He gave His only begotten Son, that whoever believes in Him should not perish but have everlasting life.*"

My, how I love Jesus for what He has done for us all. I must ask—*do you?*

I saw witnesses coming forth bearing false testimony against Him. Somehow, I could perceive the heart of those who sent for them, reasoning, "He will do away with our livelihood in the house of God! On no, not that! He needs to be stopped at any cost."

Jesus was slapped. Spat upon with contempt. Beaten and mocked. For doing good and telling the truth. I heard slanderous words about Jesus spoken to the crowds to make all believe their propaganda was real.

He was despised and rejected by men, a man of sorrows and acquainted with grief; and as one from whom men hide their faces he was despised, and we esteemed him not (Isaiah 53:3 ESV).

It was like looking into the past through a cloudy haze. Jesus was led to Herod's council, where they tried to provoke Him to dance to their tune. I could hear their thoughts: "Do a sign, wonder, or miracle for us." Their motive was clear: "Become our servant, grant us what we please; we're in charge, not You!"

The scene changed. Jesus was dragged, beaten, and treated with scorn and then led to the governing authorities to be outlawed and put to death. For what?

For revealing the heart of God, who is good to all, abundant in mercy. Who is slow to anger, granting time to repent. Who gives good news to those crushed in life. Who changes the course of people's lives by freeing them of the darkness inside. Who opens blind eyes, heals, and provides.

Surely he has borne our griefs and carried our sorrows; yet we esteemed him stricken, smitten by God, and afflicted (Isaiah 53:4 ESV).

I heard and saw the crack of a whip. Snap! Flesh flew in the air, drops of blood sprayed and ran off His back onto the floor. Here's a splintery wooden cross to bear. Move it, buster, down the Via Dolorosa, the painful way. No more of You.

But he was pierced for our transgressions; he was crushed for our iniquities; upon him was the chastisement that brought us peace, and with his wounds we are healed (Isaiah 53:5 ESV).

He walked Calvary's road bearing the beam. Some in the crowd wept as they witnessed what humanity really thinks of goodness, truth, and life. However, most cheered and mocked and heckled and spat. Not much has changed today, has it?

Jesus was walking a short distance in front of me. Then I saw how they made a crown of thorns and jammed it tightly upon His head. Blood trickled down. He could not wipe off the flow of blood and sweat.

It sounds strange, but I could hear the collective heart of those there: "Oh, we don't want a king like Him ruling over us, stopping us from doing as we please. Jam it harder down upon His head. Harder!"

I heard the hammering, the pain as the spikes were driven into His hands and feet. With a thud, the cross was rammed home in its place.

> By oppression and judgment he was taken away; and as for his generation, who considered that he was cut off out of the land of the living, stricken for the transgression of my people? (Isaiah 53:8 ESV)

Jesus cried out through wrenching pain, "Father, forgive them for they know not what they do!"

Jesus did not cry out for Himself but for us. A cry of intercession. We do not recognize how we betray, neglect, abandon, scheme, lie, put people on trial in or minds, bear false judgments, or the real effect this has on others. However, the cross reveals it all.

> Yet it was the will of the Lord to crush him; he has put him to grief; when his soul makes an offering for

guilt, he shall see his offspring; he shall prolong his days; the will of the Lord shall prosper in his hand (Isaiah 53:10 ESV).

"Father, forgive them for they know not what they do!"

The intent of His words became clear to me. It was as though He was crying out, "Let Your wrath fall upon Me. For I willingly take their punishment, so justly deserved. Let it be on Me. Father, for this purpose I came unto this hour, for You so loved this world."

> *Jesus cried out with a loud voice, saying, "Eli, Eli, lama sabachthani?" that is, "My God, My God, why have You forsaken Me?"* (Matthew 27:46 NKJV)

The answer is found in the events prior to the cross and at the scene of the crucifixion. This is what humanity is like.

We don't want to see it. Nor do we want to face the facts of betrayal, abandonment, dividing up what belongs to others, power trips, mocking, scoffing, lying, and so much more and how they affect those victimized. Jesus bore God's wrath in our place and then forgives those who see what they are really like on the inside.

> *As a result of the anguish of His soul, He will see it and be satisfied; by His knowledge the Righteous One, My Servant, will justify the many, as He will bear their wrongdoings* (Isaiah 53:11 NASB).

Jesus cried amidst such darkness, "Tetelestai, it is finished." Paid in full. Done.

All we like sheep have gone astray; we have turned, every one, to his own way; and the Lord has laid on Him the iniquity of us all (Isaiah 53:6 NKJV).

A sinless God could only legally, by the covenant law of atonement, place the iniquity of us all through the hands of human beings who literally confessed and laid hands on Him, all proven by the events leading to the crucifixion.

Yes, Jesus was betrayed into the hands of sinners (see Matthew 26:45). That aspect of the gospel is rarely taught anymore. The gospel, the living Word of God become flesh, truly reveals the thoughts and intents of the human heart (see John 1:1-14; Hebrews 4:12-13). Think about it.

Three days later Jesus rose from the dead. The heavy stone that sealed His tomb rolled away, paving the way into eternal life so we can escape the final death that awaits (see Revelation 20:11-15). For God so loved!

Can you cry out, "Father, forgive me. Now I see—take me, I am Yours. You are faithful; I am not. Please change me!"

The light from the end of the corridor brightly outlined the presence of Jesus. I followed, so humbled. He did this for such an ungrateful one like me so I could finally see my truest need. Then, I entered the light seen beyond the corridor.

CHAPTER THIRTEEN

THE GLORIOUS LAND

"I am the door. If anyone enters by Me, he will be saved, and will go in and out and find pasture."

—John 10:9 NKJV

As I exited, I was instantly engulfed in brilliant light exposing a magnificent land whose atmosphere felt like living, liquid love, a love I had never known before. Jesus turned, smiled, and then motioned me and said, "Come."

I cannot express all that Jesus spoke.

He simply pointed to things as we walked. He knew my mind, my heart. His comments, questions, laughter, and great joy refined my confidence in His great faithfulness proven by the cross! Heaven, a land of liquid love. That's how it felt—so beautiful, beyond anything we know here on earth. No human words can adequately describe it.

An unpaved road came into view. It was made of fine, golden gravel that soothed my feet as I walked upon it. We moved a short distance off the lane and stood on a slight rise. There was a grand city way off in the distance. Oddly, in an instant I knew where every building was and what was stored in each.

Likewise, intuitively, I knew my way around this glorious land. The whole place warmed my heart with a great peace. God's love engulfed my soul there.

The trees had no imperfections; the colors were outstanding. The light that filled the sky was from God. The flowers—wow, the flowers! *Amazing.* To me, it was as though all the landscape literally resounded forth aspects of God's glorious nature. He is true in all His ways and deeds! Holy, holy, holy is He!

I stood transfixed, drinking it all in, this land bathed in an atmosphere of liquid love. I knew Jesus was standing nearby. Sometimes I thought I lost sight of Him, but His presence filled this place. "Look and see!" He said with a smile.

Turning toward the gate's exit, I saw saints of God emerging into the most stunningly beautiful, glorious meadow where we stood. The grass was perfect with unbendable blades. You never bent a blade. It felt so good. Magnificent trees were spaced here and there. Off in the distance, a forest beckoned. From the nearby road, others branched into the depths of heaven.

All who exited the gate began to walk in different directions into this field. I drank it all in. A man entered the field along the road. He spied his father, who had died years before, coming toward him. The man was shocked to see his father approaching him.

I instantly knew why and what happened. His dad was distant and abrasive. They had gotten into an argument because he tried to witness to his father. The man became so angry at his dad's response and name-calling that he walked away, holding a grudge built by years of strife and emotional neglect.

As years passed, he would not return his father's calls or read his many letters. His siblings told him, "Dad has cancer from all those years of smoking and drinking." Even at that, he refused to see his father.

Now his father neared and spoke, "Hi son, when the cancer took hold, before I passed I recalled your words to call on Jesus.

I did and you were right. Thank you, son!" The man melted as they embraced. "I've always been so proud of you. I am so sorry for not saying that to you. Jesus cleansed me of my pride—all my hay, wood, and stubble gone."

They both wept. Even before their tears dried, all sorrow and regrets were gone. All undone things finalized. Healing prevailed in this land of liquid love. As they walked away, both appeared like they were in the prime of life without defects—no more faults.

A godly couple who had just passed entered together. A crowd led by a very young child approached them. The child had died from a tragic car wreck, but the driver survived. It was the couple's son and he said, "Hi, Mom, Dad!"

He then grew before their eyes. They embraced. All heartache gone. All that longing graciously expunged.

Other believing relatives and friends who had passed on before met them. At first, they appeared as they remembered each other to be. Then all transformed into what they looked like in their prime of life, around 30 years old, without defect or blemish. They proceeded into heaven's land to a place prepared. All who entered were believers. Everyone there walked their own crimson way with its joys and sorrows, sufferings and sadness along with its happier and joyous times.

I saw some who had just died for their faith. They were met by those who had gone on before. They moved on to a place where a joyous reception awaits.

Others I saw had died of disease. All entered healed. They were transformed into the prime of life with no flaws, again appearing to be around 30 years old.

Amazing were the children entering there. I looked and Jesus was greeting them as they ran to Him. He bent down to embrace them, removing all fear as he played and romped with them a bit. He was tossing and catching some of them like a loving father would with his little ones.

Then the most amazing thing transpired. A woman walked through the gate and entered the field. She saw an infant crawling to her. The child became an adult before her eyes, and he smiled and said, "Hi Mom, no worries, I came here."

She burst out weeping healing tears because this one was one she aborted out of great fear. The clinic was so sterile. She remembered what she had done with deep guilt. She became born again, but the guilt gnawed at her soul.

Her son said, "Mom, recall you're forgiven. We now have time to play. Let's go, come."

Hand in hand they went. Guilt and tears were removed and her conscience cleansed. I called this area near the gate "the field of reunion." Where things are settled. Healing occurs, tears are dried, while sorrow is removed and all is replaced with great joy in this land of liquid love. All return to life as God intended it to be from the beginning before the foundation of the world.

There was Jesus with all the young children jumping about, playing, showing Him things and then me as well. Jesus smiled, and the children giggled and laughed. Other souls appeared along with angelic beings. Some were folks who were never able to have children. They gathered the children together and joyfully escorted them into the depths of Beulah Land.

* * *

I spoke into the studio's big microphone, "Still to this day, I can imagine when the disciples wanted to brush away from Jesus the children whom their parents sent to be blessed. He probably blessed them that day, like I saw there, gathering them around with joy, probably romping on the ground with them."

"I can imagine that too," said Tina. "Being a mother I can!"

"As a dad, I see that as well. When my kids were small, they loved it when I gently tossed and caught them," Ryder replied, adding, "Yeah, the disciples remind me of some folks today."

"Why's that?" I asked.

"When Jesus answered them, He said, 'Let the little children come for theirs is the kingdom of heaven.' After all, according to the Bible, as Isaiah 55:8-11 and Isaiah 46:10 point out, God will perform the word He speaks."

Tina: "Oh my, I can see the phone lines and text messages lighting up with those who disagree."

"Yes," I replied, "for little kids and for developmentally disabled folks who have not reached that age of accountability, heaven's doors are opened wide to them."

"Why is that, B.W.?"

"First off, Jesus said not to forbid such to enter. Next, children are teachable. It is easy for them to believe, because the live only in the present, and I am sure in heaven they are trained very well, and all restored.

"Some people think their way is the only way or they twist the meaning of scriptures. My guess is that the Ephesus-type people do stray away from their first love in exchange for carnal things. They exalt man's opinion over God's, thinking these are of God, but they are not."

"Thank you so much, dear Jesus. My husband and I lost our first child; she passed at three, fever," Tina said as she sniffled, fighting back the tears. We had to take an impromptu station break.

You know, we have fallen a long way from the promises of God and the treasures held for us in heaven.

CHAPTER FOURTEEN

LOVE DEEP, WIDE, UNFATHOMABLE

"And we have known and believed the love that God has for us. God is love, and he who abides in love abides in God, and God in him."

—1 John 4:16 NKJV

Happy little children smiled and frolicked about as they were escorted into the depths of heaven's land with no more worries, hurts, or pain. All fears were removed and minds purified by simple faith in the grace of Christ.

Jesus smiled as we walked back toward the golden pathway that meandered through this beautiful, undulating, love-drenched terrain toward a forest residing in a calm swale. The great city could be seen off to the right in the distance.

I looked around. People exited the gate where all things were made new and unsaid things resolved. They met loved ones who had gone on before. Waves of mercy and compassion dried every tear and removed all sorrow. Everything was made new.

This stunningly peaceful, calming meadow, this field of reunion, surrounded us. Blades of perfectly formed grass glistened with life. The blades of grass did not bend and were not crushed as we walked. Flowers and every plant in this grand meadowland by the gate radiated God's love so much that it felt as if these very plants were singing! Yes, there were songbirds there, many.

Does this mean animals have souls? No, it does not. If God wants animals there, why not? He is God and can do what pleases Him. Animals are there. They do not have the same functions as they do on earth. They are for God's good pleasure. I never saw any reptiles there. Many of these animals are like those seen on earth; others are not. Their purpose is for those who love animals, to help take care of them without the mess and the fuss.

All things in heaven are for God's good pleasure. He rejoices over the pleasure of His beloved children. I can imagine what it was like when God stood next to Adam as he named the animals.

Heaven is the place we were designed for. However, humanity fell. Jesus came to reconcile us back to God. At that final restoration of all things, we will help the Lord take care of His precious creation with no thought of rebellion ever again. How? All who enter have been sealed to receive this great inheritance just as Ephesians 1:3-14 says.

Heaven is a busy place, like a working vacation. There is plenty of time for rest, because there, what you do is restful in and of itself. I will share more on this as we go.

As we walked, I looked around drinking in the love of God. In the sky above, I noticed several great heavenly creatures flying about. Some did not have wings but rode on what looked like wheels of spinning light. Others soared on uniquely crafted wings of light. Angelic beings were many.

This field, to me, was a place where one gets acclimated to the land of God's liquid love. Here one is introduced to his or her real purpose for being. It is a place where all trauma is erased.

There is no sin, no sickness, no regret here, only a profound joy of coming into a union of close fellowship with God that was lost in the Garden of Eden. John 17 describes the love of God, how it unites us who believe in Christ back to our purpose and His will before the fall.

Do we really think we know what love is? I do not mean the emotional kind, brotherly love, or a family type of love, but the Love that God has. Can we even begin to fathom its unfathomable deepness?

Paul prayed in Ephesians 3:14-19 that we should search it out. So what is stopping us?

* * *

Tina inquired, "Is there really any way we can define God's love, get our head wrapped around it? There is so much confusion about God's love. There are even those who claim that God's love allows anything because it is simply unconditional. The love there in heaven, B.W., how would you describe it?"

I replied, "Seeing this place sent me on an ongoing quest to try to define what God's agape love means. *Agape* is the Greek word for love, a specific type. That's what I felt in heaven's land where the atmosphere was like liquid love. I have tried explaining it here, in this current now, which is most difficult."

Ryder interjected, "Why is that?"

I continued, "The meaning of agape love, in my opinion, has been watered down in modern Christian circles to a one-size-fits-all, simple definition of unconditional love. It may be unconditional, but it is not without standards. I ask, does unconditional love mean it is so totally without conditions that anything goes and must be accepted, or is there more to it than just that?

"In military terms, unconditional surrender means to lay down one's armaments, placing oneself entirely at the mercy of the one surrendered to. So, there are standards attached to the term *unconditional*, aren't there?

"Nevertheless, some people interject their own subjective opinions of what love is. For example, God's love in many places is interpreted to justify that God will not hold anyone to account, that all will somehow universally be allowed into heaven. It does not matter what you do or believe, they reason. But I ask: how can true love be without standards?

"They reason that God's love is without conditions and therefore change the Greek meaning of 1 John 4:8 to read this: 'Love is God.' However, the reality from the original Greek text of 1 John 4:8 translates like this: "God, as to His nature, loves." See the difference?"

* * *

After I returned from this experience, I began a quest to explain what God's agape love means. I searched the etymology of the Greek word *agape/agapao* (love) and how it was translated in both the Hebrew and Latin Bible text. From this, I discovered a meaning for agape love that has substance and that will help uncover what this word means in the Bible.

I also discovered that there are shades of meaning for God's agape love. How it is used in the Bible pinpoints one or more of agape's shades of meaning. With that, let me give you the first meaning of agape love:

1. It means unconditional cherishing, nurturing, taking care of, and chastening in order to restore.

How so? Look at it this way: God's love cherishes, nurtures, and takes care of the world. He keeps animals and feeds and houses them. They find a home. He makes the rain fall on the just and unjust. God unconditionally cherishes, nurtures, and provides for all, saints and sinners alike. After all, the earth is the Lord's and the fulness thereof, right?

Next, His love chastens, disciplines, rebukes, and reproves in order to reconcile the wayward back to Himself as well as separate the wheat from the chaff, the real from the fake.

Let me add this first definition into John 3:16 (NKJV): "*For God so loved* [cherished, nurtured, took care of, chastened in order to restore] *the world that He gave his only begotten Son, that whoever believes in Him* [in His faithfulness seen on the cross] *should not perish but have everlasting life.*"

Now read the rest of John 3:17-21 (NIV). Do you see it?

> *For God did not send his Son into the world to condemn the world, but to save the world through him. Whoever believes in him is not condemned, but whoever does not believe stands condemned already because they have not believed in the name of God's one and only Son. This is the verdict: Light has come into the world, but people loved darkness instead of light because their deeds were evil. Everyone who does evil hates the light and will not come into the light for fear that their deeds will be exposed. But whoever lives by the truth comes into the light, so that it may be seen plainly that what they have done has been done in the sight of God.*

CHAPTER FIFTEEN

A BOX OF NAILS

"You will guide me with Your counsel, and afterward receive me to glory. Whom have I in heaven but You?"
—Psalm 73:24-25 NKJV

We stood near an intersection. Here, Jesus, smiled and motioned toward the grand city seen in the great distance, then toward a great forest beckoning ahead. He was asking me, "Which would you like?" I knew the answer before I even could speak. It was like a good-natured repartee.

I answered, "The land, the countryside."

We moved toward the great forest with much repartee between us. Amidst all this He, the Lord of glory, was walking with me as my friend just as He walked with Moses and spoke to him as a friend. The compassion and love Jesus has is amazing. We walked along the way. The scenery changed from meadowland to areas where buildings could be seen surrounded by what looked to me like a park.

The buildings were surrounded by beautiful trees and flowers, all well placed and perfectly spaced. All the trees and flowers were alive with the most stunning colors and fragrances.

The fragrances of heaven are unlike anything here on earth. There is life and texture to the scent of heaven's flowers, fields, the whole atmosphere. It invigorates you, reminding you of the love of God and that all things were created for His great pleasure and will. Along the way, within these park-like areas, people were sitting on the ground, listening to some old saint whom the world may have forgotten. I was reminded of the teaching and learning we get in school but here it was outdoors, in living color.

To get an idea of what I mean, imagine that the one who was speaking was Onesimus, or Justus, or Aristarchus whom Paul mentions in Colossians 4:7-18. Imagine hearing the girl named Rhoda who heard and saw Peter after his miraculous release from prison but left him standing outside the door. We don't hear about her after that—what's her story?

Now, I did not see any of these folks, but I use them to illustrate the caliber of people who were speaking and sharing their stories. These stories revolved around the suffering some endured for Christ and the crimes committed against them. Some were raped by enemies of God. Others were tortured for their faith. Others had a good life.

This may sound strange to you, that people in heaven were telling their stories, but try to understand that all pain, suffering, trauma, and anguish are removed upon arrival. What was being revealed here was what gave each their ability to endure and overcome every crisis they went through—it was their trust alone in God's great faithfulness that got them through all the things thrown at them by the sin-ravaged world.

What I saw being taught and expressed was the sovereign nature of God's faithfulness that makes all things new. As they spoke, their life stories unfolded before my eyes. I saw clearly what many are blind to here on earth—the faithfulness of God.

This old world is not our home. God is faithful to get us through all things. Thus, I ask you, will you trust God when you have problems?

What we go through here on earth is nothing compared to the glory of heaven that awaits. This old world is fallen. God will make all things new. His nature of love will justly remove the dross to protect those whom He reconciles back to Himself by what Jesus accomplished on the cross (see Mark 14:41; Colossians 2:15; Hebrews 12:3).

Often, many in this life truly become the hands and feet of Christ, tasked to expose the true nature of the human heart and still offer forgiveness to all for what we do to each other, our own selves, and even God.

As each spoke, they exemplified how they were treated here on earth by those who claim that their ways, tolerances, and love is superior but who are proven wrong. As each spoke, I could see what they went through and learned. This is precisely what Romans 8:38-39 speaks about: nothing can separate us from the love of God, no matter what happens to us here.

Listening to them was like having Romans 8:35-39 come alive. Right there they were, revealing how tribulation, distress, persecution, famine, nakedness, peril, and persecution could not separate them, or us, from God's love.

One thing that impressed me about this is how God sovereignly allows such things to expose the nature and deceptive enchantments of evil. Evil is unequivocally used to gain authoritarian control over all by justifying all that is evil and crucifying all that is decent and good to create a "better, more perfect" world. The Bible tells us that vengeance belongs to the Lord. He will repay. We offer forgiveness. They offer reparations and justify theft of what one rightfully owns.

God is faithful—He will repay. Like Jesus, we extend freedom to our enemies so they may change in ways we never anticipate. By this, the guilty can repent, or if not, they are justly condemned.

All in all, those who told their biographies revealed how they were prepared by the Lord to expose the works of the devil and his spiritual minions that will be used to testify against them at an appointed time just as Daniel 7:9-12 reveals.

God's faithfulness was being extolled and revealed here. All marveled at the wisdom and ways God showed His heartfelt love and never-ending devotion. I heard, as we passed by, former persecutors who came to Jesus after seeing they were on the wrong side. Some were amazed and repented: "What love and devotion they have for God and each other—forgive me, oh Lord, for what I have done to these people!"

As they spoke, you could see such weeping as God's faithful assembly forgave them and accepted them as their own despite what they had done to others.

For I am persuaded that neither death nor life, nor angels nor principalities nor powers, nor things present nor things to come, nor height nor depth, nor any other created thing, shall be able to separate us from the love of God which is in Christ Jesus our Lord (Romans 8:38-39 NKJV).

Here, I began learning what Hebrews 11:32-40 speaks about—trusting in God's faithfulness gets us through all storms of life. That gets us through good times as well as all the bad in ways most never realize till they arrive here.

Some who spoke revealed a crisis of faith. Others lived every day for Jesus and not for the world. They described the personal battles they faced. Even when tears were shed and God's answer to prayer was "no," they understood. They laughed, smiled, and the listeners were amazed at the depths of God's faithfulness. Many who spoke were also blessed by God, but they never experienced persecution. They revealed how they were used by God in ways they never knew, which demonstrates how God links events and people together.

So you can get the idea of what I mean, I will use this simple illustration: one saintly believer, a Sunday school teacher, used to be easily angered by delays. God used a box of nails to mend his heart. Before that, across the world a young toddler, along with his parents, was fleeing a revolution ravaged land. In the process, both mother and father died and the child was left alone, crying beside the road. Meanwhile a woman was having a crisis of faith due to what she experienced in church: "How could they? Who needs Christians?"

The Sunday school teacher was stopped by red light after red light. His frustration grew. Then, unexpected road construction caused him to fume and curse all the more. Unbeknownst to him, along the road a construction worker dropped a box of nails on the road, saying, "Oh well, ain't my problem," and walked away.

The infuriated Sunday school teacher suddenly pulled off the road with a flat tire, "God, all I'm doing is trying to serve You. Why all this? I'll be late!" He fixed the flat and tossed the car jack back into the car.

The woman who was having a crisis was driving and contemplating the futility of her life when a nail entered her tire. She had no choice but to pull up behind the man, who was slamming the trunk of his car after fixing his tire. He saw her look of distress and asked cautiously, "Do you need help?" She was thinking he needed to just spin off and leave her to fend for herself. After all, he was on a mission from God!

She replied, "Yes, I have a flat."

He changed her tire. These two tire changes ruined his suit but got the notice of the women. "Did I inconvenience you?"

"No, no problem," he said with a pleasant smile. "I'll make it to church when I get there."

"What church is that?"

"New Hope Baptist, ma'am."

She drove away thinking, *There's a real believer after all. New Hope, hmmm.*

That event changed her life. She joined New Hope. Later she went on a missions trip to help rescue recently orphaned children at a refugee camp. The influence she had on one child who lost his parents in the attempt to flee was amazing. He later became a minister and brought countless souls to Christ.

What about the guy who deliberately left the nails on the road? Well, he rejected Christ no matter what and spilled more than just nails in people's lives. But regardless, God uses all things for His good.

The Sunday school teacher learned he needed to work on his anger and was freed. The woman's faith was restored, affecting one orphan who later grew to change the lives of many. All came forth by a box of nails that God worked together for His good in ways unseen.

This typifies the types of stories I heard. Heaven truly unpacks all the whys and "why me" moments we have in life, unveiling God's faithfulness getting us through it all and causing a deeper love for God.

You saw how they overcame, all in living history. All rejoiced seeing God's great faithfulness play out. Hearing them speak was like gaining a full understanding of the faithfulness of God that causes one to shout His praises.

Those who spoke—I have no clue who they were. The majority were just folks like you and me who think they do so little for the kingdom of God. Then a trial of faith comes, refining our character and changing our tune (see Romans 8:28-30).

Some overcame addictions and family issues, like unsaved loved ones. Others revealed how they were blessed abundantly by God and still held fast to the faithfulness of God by not letting it go to their heads.

Everyone was speaking and listening to the glorified Christ Jesus, not themselves. Each boasted in Christ alone—how about you?

This memory later helped lead me to grasp the second definition of God's agape love I uncovered from my research. Recall the first definition for God's agape love:

1. Agape love unconditionally cherishes, nurtures, provides for all. Unconditionally means without our conditions and ways of interfering.

First John 4:8 reveals that God's nature is one that loves. The feeling of love itself is not our god, but rather it is God's nature and character to love. Therefore, the work that the Holy Spirit does is likewise a reflection of God's nature to love, which seen in this second definition:

2. Agape love teaches us to be sensitive to the Holy Spirit. The Holy Spirit helps us by guiding, explaining, and coming alongside to aid, comfort, and equip, teaching us to walk according to His truth and not our own.

The Holy Spirit is called the Helper, one sent to come alongside to aid and comfort. He leads us into all truth. He teaches and instructs us, guides us, equips us, tells us things to come.

Through the gifts of the Spirit, He establishes us in the faith, teaching us how to live responsibly before God and each other, even using a box of nails when needed, so we stop the devil from setting up shop in our lives and enslaving us.

When chastened by the Lord, we learn that God loves us enough to teach us right from wrong no matter how much we fuss and scream or how many boxes of nails it takes. While we bemoan, *God, this is not according to my conditions! Wahh wahh, I want it my way!* then the chastening comes. The door then finally shuts to the devil having his way in your life.

In this second definition of agape love, you learn that you belong to Him and that He is faithful. You can't be separated from His great love no matter what comes your way. We learn what it means to be His and become less of a slave to our sins than we were the day before.

God is faithful to keep His word even though it may not be in the way we think or like.

* * *

We continued along the way. Pathways branched off the road, leading to other places specially prepared for His beloved people. As we walked, Jesus was with me and then He wasn't, yet I felt His presence everywhere as though He had never left. This is way too hard to explain in this mortal sphere in which we live. I began to grasp, ever so slowly, that what He said about never leaving or forsaking us is true in ways we often neglect to notice in this mortal life.

Jesus was affable, conversing with each person we came across like they were His only ones. When He speaks, that is what it is like—He speaks directly to you. His love is so real, tangible, and personable at the same time. However, I was not allowed to converse with any person there. I could listen but not speak. I was at peace about this and understood why. Such things can make a person's brain become so full of themselves that they soon stink. I came away from my after death and heaven experience with a strong aversion to my own human pride. We all face that temptation every day on this earth.

Thus, for me, it was okay not to converse with anyone. Such conversing could cause a violation of the boundaries of God's protective love. We have folks who claim that they take daily trips to heaven to bring back messages from the deceased to living relatives and friends on earth. Necromancy is not allowed. It is a violation of God's protective boundaries and loving standards of the royal law of love written in the heart. May they repent and stop this before it is too late. Those who do this are not seeing heaven but are instead in contact with deceivers. Is your faith in God's faithfulness, or more in them? You decide.

Have you noticed how swell headed some folks can be about such things? Why is that allowed? God tests and refines the heart. The word of God reveals the thoughts and intents of the human heart in more ways than one. Often it is what others see that reveals their need to repent. Amen!

As we walked, we came across grasslands. In the distance I saw some of the patriarchs mentioned in the Bible. I could not make out who they were—their abodes were large but simple. They resembled the boxy, angular shapes of the pueblos of Taos, New Mexico. Many of the buildings or abodes I encountered in heaven looked similar in shape. Their walls reminded me of a golden stucco-like substance. They were stunningly beautiful to behold. One cannot, in our current here and now, replicate their shapes and design. I do not think there is enough building material in any country in the world to make some of these.

What I noticed is that people lived in the same area with those they influenced for Christ in any small, hidden, or large way. You were able to visit them as often as you or they liked. No one ever tired of visitors or visiting. I joke with modern-day folks on this—no texting, no cellphones in heaven, no internet, no distractions—all visited face to face. Sadly, for many, such human interaction has become a forgotten art form. Tragically, this leads to loss of hope and suicide. But that is one reason Jesus has His church where you can seek fellowship so your heart will slowly and gently be mended.

People who reside in heaven are in their spiritual bodies. Adults all appear about 30 years old, in the prime of life, no flaws or bad-hair days. They retain human features, yet the sexual reproduction mechanisms we have here on earth are not there in heaven. There is no need for these or the features used to reproduce. Women look like women and men look like men; the way God designed us to be.

In the New Testament, and hinted at in the Old, there is the resurrection of the physical body. That has not happened yet. For now, those in Christ enter heaven in their spiritual bodies, along with their purified souls. The Bible describes a "later time" when our spiritual being is united with our new body.

Why is this? God keeps His word. We were designed with a spirit, soul, and body. At the Resurrection those whom Christ made righteous in His sight will receive a new body for the new heavens and earth to come.

He made us a certain way, and that way will be restored at an appointed time when there is no longer sin and rebellion. A time when all things are made new and the old has passed away (see Revelation 21 and 22).

> *I know that whatever God does, it shall be forever. Nothing can be added to it, and nothing taken from it. God does it, that men should fear before Him* (Ecclesiastes 3:14 NKJV).

CHAPTER SIXTEEN

PLANTINGS OF THE LORD

"Let the field be joyful, and all that is in it. Then all the trees of the woods will rejoice before the Lord."
—Psalm 96:12-13 NKJV

Everything was alive. Crisp and clear. Every hill, swale, plant, and tree seemed to be rejoicing, displaying the goodness of the Lord! Everything was fruitful and abundant.

As strange as this sounds, the plants, trees, and flowers were singing, each in its own pleasant way reflecting the Lord's greatness. I could see animals off in the distance—magnificent, perfect animals.

Time as we know it has no meaning there. This was eternal time. That sense of it has never left me to this very day. Because of it, I don't long for temporary, unimportant belongings. These desires are foreign to me.

This sense of eternal time has helped me overcome anxieties, fears, doubts, and still does, like it did in 1988. I had just gotten married. My parents were visiting. We were walking around the neighborhood. I lost my business due to cutthroat competition. I lost my employees and I had recently bought a house.

The responsibility of being a godly, kingdom-minded man, tasked to care for his wife and family, weighed heavily on me. How could I? After all, I "lost" the means of support. How could I provide for her? The house—would I be able to keep it?

My wife and my mother ambled ahead of my father and me. Then my dad looked at me, grabbed my hand and shoulder, and said, "Son, I am proud of you."

I thought, fighting back the tears, *How could you? My business collapsed. I'm married, I'm failing, and I can't find a job.*

Then the sense of eternal time brought it home to me in an instant kaleidoscope of truth. God is faithful. He just healed the rift I had with my dad, causing me to try to perform for approval. I melted and was healed that day.

That is what heaven is like—our heavenly Father saying, "Well done!" as we cry, "I failed, look at me!" Then the rift between us and our heavenly Father is healed and all the raw deals in life fade away.

Eternal time sets things in perspective when we lose sight of how great the Lord God Almighty really is. Eternal time helps us view the world differently. It is like what Hebrews 11 says— we are strangers in this land, just passing through, seeking a heavenly homeland. As we long for heaven, the things of this earth will fade away, but the faithful love of God never fails. The hardships in this life are fleeting.

There I was in heaven, drinking it all in as we peacefully walked along this country lane. The forest lay ahead. What a grand forest! What abundant trees spaced apart, causing the scenery to blend, mix, and match perfectly. The forests are my kind of place. I love exploring and hiking in areas few dare to tread. Nothing on earth can adequately compare with the forests in heaven. Imagine the giant redwoods and the most pristine forest you ever saw combined with awesome underbrush that does not impede movement. Multiply that by one thousand to the trillionth power and that hardly compares to the beauty of this forest.

We met others walking in the woodland, following various paths going in different directions. They would stop and speak to the Lord a bit. Two women approached us. They smiled and joyfully asked the Lord if it would be okay for them to tell me who they were. "No, not now," was the joyous answer—like, *Not now, but later, decidedly yes*, and then a smile.

As I said, I was at peace about this. After all, heaven with its eternal time was healing my heart from the haunting memory of hell, which triggered me. I also had terrifying dreams. I had PTSD and did not even know it. After this visit to heaven, I could handle the memories.

That is the reason Jesus revealed to me a small patch of heaven. As for the two ladies, I have no clue who they were. Other people walked by with brief but joyful hellos and greetings. They understood my time was yet to come. For now, simple welcomes and hellos were just fine.

Heaven reflects forth the glory of God's full nature and character. Such knowledge cannot be uttered, and it must remain so till you get there. Heaven is designed in such a way to bring God great pleasure to express His true will and character. Life on earth helps prepare us to live in such a place, sealed forever with absolutely *no* possibly ever to ever rebel again.

From the moment I entered this forest in heaven, it was clear to me that I would be helping to take care of God's precious land, rivers, streams, animals, trees and cities, and beloved people, and so much more.

God does not need angels or humanity in any regard. He is fully self-sufficient in and of Himself. Yet He has great pleasure in giving the care of His creation to those He made with intelligent reason. He likes that. He delights in involving those He created with intelligence. The Bible teaches that God involves us and His angels in helping carry out His will. Just the fact that we are called the body of Christ, to be His hands, feet, and so forth, expresses this principle very well. All things are created for His good pleasure, just as Revelation 4:11 (KJV) reveals.

There is no decay in heaven. If you like forest and rural areas in this life, you might find yourself tending to these areas, but unlike how you would on earth. The tending and keeping here brings great joy to the Lord and you as well.

Those of us who like animals will help tend to the awesome ones seen in heaven, but with no boots or shovels if you know what I mean. These animals need attention, a good brushing and romping around with, leading them here and there.

In the forest, I saw people in the trees who appeared to be helping the trees shine forth more of God's renown. I'm not sure how to explain it better than that.

This forest seemed to symbolize those who are called "trees of righteousness like the plantings of the Lord" in Isaiah 61:1-4. Those people help Him build up, repair, and restore what many generations have ruined in order to reflect His glory. The people tending these remarkable trees helped them shine forth the glory of God's character and the nature of His love in greater and greater degrees. Maybe we are all called to a similar purpose in this mortal life, causing our salt to always remain fresh and our lamps to shine unhindered.

Jesus quoted Isaiah 61:1-4 in Luke 4. The same Spirit that raised Him from the dead dwells in us. As born-again believers in Christ, we have that same Spirit, the Holy Spirit, the gift of the new birth to teach us here to be His body on earth. There is more to the Holy Spirit than having fun and playing games to get things for oneself as has been taught in many quarters of the modern church.

The memories of this forest later quite unexpectedly helped me to discover the third definition of God's agape love, the type of love in our heart by the Holy Ghost as we read about in Romans 5:5.

3. True agape love sets boundaries and teaches right from wrong, justly explaining why. It defends, protects, makes things right, brings true justice and righteousness to light; bears forth God's power to set free and heal; helps exchange heaviness for the oil of joy that comes by being accepted in the beloved.

We see this kind of love being played out in Isaiah 61:1-4 when it tells us that the Holy Spirit works through us to give good news to those whose hearts are shattered, broken, held captive, in bondage—helping them become set free. This power is on loan to us by God to shine forth *His* glory, not ours. By it, we hold evil in check, proving all aspects of God's love true. The Holy Spirit in us helps us accomplish this kind of love. How so?

The power of the gifts of the Holy Spirit mentioned in 1 Corinthians 12 is to bring forth God's justice and righteousness. Some believers pooh-pooh the nine gifts mentioned in this chapter, while others abuse these gifts and make them playthings, staining the name of the Lord.

Is it any wonder that the state of the world and church is so messed up? Some try to explain the gifts away, thereby convincing many that these gifts are no longer for today. How could the gifts disappear when the Bible in Romans 11:29 clearly tells us that God's gifts and callings are without repentance? No wonder the world is going to hell in a handbasket.

Now, what am I getting at? Let me explain. God's agape love and His righteousness and justice work hand in hand. Love influences justice and righteousness and vice versa. If you love someone, you will punish wrongdoers while at the same time offer them a chance to repent. That is how just God is. No one can convict the Lord of arbitrary selection to damnation. He shows no partiality to any. The power of His word offers a choice when none existed before.

This attribute of God's agape love will hold to account those who are truly guilty. They never realize the ruin and pain left behind. Nor do they realize how many boxes of nails they toss upon the road of life till the day of judgment comes. By then it is too late.

We are called to show His love, righteousness, and justice by helping the widows and orphans, the poor and downtrodden to better themselves, not enable them to remain in that state to be exploited. His Spirit helps us to give good news to those crushed in spirit. Have you been beaten down in life? Left in the dark? You tried church, and since that didn't work too well, you feel left in the cold. I ask the Lord that you might find a fellowship so that your hope and living responsibility to God and others is restored.

Folks, we need the spiritual gift of discernment, along with the gift of wisdom and knowledge that comes on loan to us by the Spirit of God, so we know what to do and how to correctly bring God's loving righteousness and justice to light. God's kind of love speaks with power to change lives to be more a reflection of His good, upright character and less of our fallen nature.

Without God's compassion and graciousness, the hearts of the profane would be hardened even more.

Now what do the trees of righteousness mentioned in Isaiah 61:1-4 have to do with the trees I saw in that heavenly forest, if anything at all? Isaiah 61:1-4 describes trees of righteousness as being the plantings of the Lord (you and I) who shine forth the glory of who God is and what He is about. This is important. Those living can rest under the shade of God's love that helps folks find meaning and purpose in life, attained by mending broken hearts torn apart by a sinful world.

We need the gift of faith for this task—not faith in another, but in God's faithfulness to us. Don't believe me? What does Mark 11 and 1 Corinthians 13 say about this?

> *And though I have the gift of prophecy, and understand all mysteries and all knowledge, and though I have all faith, so that I could remove mountains, but have not love, I am nothing* (1 Corinthians 13:2 NKJV).

> *So Jesus answered and said to them, "Have faith in God. For assuredly, I say to you, whoever says to this mountain, 'Be removed and be cast into the sea,' and does not doubt in his heart, but believes that those things he says will be done, he will have whatever he says"* (Mark 11:22-23 NKJV).

Mountains represent kingdoms. Faith that removes mountains involves removing kingdoms of darkness, even at the expense of laying down your own life to bring them down. Jesus did so, and those who die for Christ still do. We see this lesson entwined in all of Mark 11.

The gift of faith is for removing the darkness that keeps people away from finding the only one true God and the forgiveness He freely offers (see Mark 11:11-19). We need such faith today.

Trees of righteousness, the plantings of the Lord, help set the captives free from repeating the same mistakes and problems. We are assisted by the wisdom and discernment of the Holy Spirit to uncover deep wounds that keep us captive. Like maybe a rift between you and your dad, like the Lord did for me. *What do you have need of?*

Do you trust Him, Jesus, to mend your heart, take your hand, and slowly walk you out of the prison that binds you? May you find the plantings of the Lord to help uncover His wisdom, knowledge, discernment, and the healing that awaits so you are transformed into one yourself.

The plantings of the Lord, the trees of righteous, proclaim this is the day, the hour, to become accepted in the beloved, the Lord Jesus Christ. Come to the Lord, all you who doubt or even believe that He does not exist because of what you have seen in this fallen life. Jesus heals.

Come, you who are weary and tired, beaten down in life! It's time to make it right between you and God by accepting what He has already done for you on the cross.

God plants us as His trees of righteousness to declare that the day of God's vengeance is at hand, so you can return to the Lord and do just as Isaiah 61:1-4 says.

This is why the gift of true prophecy is so important. You need to know the seasons of God's timetable. We need prophetic words that cut to the heart and change the direction when one is heading toward destruction, not just pleasant words used to justify the trip.

There comes a day when the profane with their prideful, arrogant, prancing ways will see what they betrayed, abandoned, and treated with contempt. Some say, "If God is all-loving then He must love what I love and hate what I hate," but that's not the way it works. But they contend: "How could love ever unleash wrath and vengeance against anyone? That's not love." My answer—you do not know the nature of love. Go into the wilderness and try petting a mama bear's cub and you'll learn there is vengeance involved in agape love.

Yes, His love will plead for your return while you do as you please, but touch any of God's beloved and you will be met with wrath. Keep living as you do—the whirlwind is what you'll reap for how you treated the gift of life He gave you.

The Lord God says of vengeance that He will repay. What you sow, you will reap. His love keeps calling you home. If you keep twisting His standards meant to protect us and keep us out of the devil's den, then He will separate you into the place you really don't want to go—forever.

God makes all things right in the end.

I am glad God's agape love is like that. He offers forgiveness to all in such a manner that divides the wheat from the chaff, so the wheat will finally be safe from all the chaff.

Trees of righteousness, the plantings of the Lord, are called to expose evil, called to account. Called to intercede with others, praying against a host of spiritual darkness. Those who love God should love others enough to intercede.

We are in a great spiritual war. And when this war gets hot, we may be called to use great discernment. In World War II, many discovered a deeper need to fight for family and home against human minions gone mad with power and greed. God's love protects and fights against darkness in many ways. Prepare yourself.

Amidst all this, people need the oil of God's gladness to erase the heaviness and despair we feel. God's love does that—brings His hope, justice, and righteousness back into the land.

We need the gift of languages as well to articulate and pray for these things, not for contentious "what ifs" and "can't be." The plantings of the Lord help rebuild what many generations have destroyed and help make these new, a place resounding forth the majesty of the agape love of God.

God's love sets boundaries and standards, revealing what is right and wrong and why. By this, His love gently guides us to learn to love what He loves and hate what He hates. Any type of love that refuses to set boundaries and standards is not love at all. That kind of love produces slavery leading to death, destruction, and theft. We provide for, train, and protect our own children. Then why can't God for His own adopted ones?

God reveals this in the Bible. There are only children of the devil, darkness, and wrath, and then there are His adopted. True, all humans are His created beings, but not all those created are actually His. May the lost reach forth and find Him (see Acts 17:26-30).

The Holy Spirit sheds abroad the love of God into our hearts, thus teaching us the necessity and importance of the boundaries His great love provides. In this life we learn truth from error, right from wrong. We learn the importance of God's protective boundaries by learning *in this life* what it is like to live outside His boundaries. There is no other way for a just God to accomplish this without *going contrary to His own nature and character.* God cannot deny Himself (see 2 Timothy 2:13; Hebrews 6:18).

In fact, this is seen in God's word where the prophets and even the law teach there are boundaries. Cross these and it was not good for ancient Israel (see Isaiah 1:18-20). God always offered grace to return till the time when such remedy was rejected, as 2 Chronicles 36:15-16 reveals.

What happens to a nation that forgets God? God sends a warning, like He did through Jonah to Nineveh (see Jonah 3:1-10). If they listen, they'll be spared. If not, they won't.

By this God's people learn *why* to hate what God hates and love what God loves because the *why* is lived through. This life prepares us for the next (see Revelation 21:4-7).

The power of the gospel sets hearts free—not our works. We who are His own are to reflect just who God really is and what He is like to a world desperately in need of His healing touch upon their broken lives and hearts. Over our time on earth, we learn how to forsake the ways of the flesh, the world, and the devil in the process. Oh, the depths of God's agape love!

1. Love that unconditionally cherishes, nurtures, takes care of, and chastens in order to restore without our conditions getting in the way.

2. Love that teaches responsibility by guiding, helping, training, equipping, explaining, coming alongside to aid, bring comfort, and teaching us to walk according to God's truth, learning His ways and standards and how to not live by our own.

3. Agape love is a love that defends, protects, sets boundaries, and reveals what is right and wrong and why. Agape love makes things right, brings forth true justice, and

bears forth God's power to heal and set people free. Agape love helps exchange one's heaviness for the oil of joy that comes by revealing your unconditional acceptance in the beloved.

CHAPTER SEVENTEEN

A GLORIOUS INHERITANCE!

"So Jesus answered and said to them, 'Have faith in God.'"
—Mark 11:22 NJKV

Tina asked, "How do we become more like the tree of His righteousness and less Laodicean-like?"

I replied, "Great question. From a hindsight perspective, this involves a process that often entails going through fiery trials, which teach us to trust completely in the faithfulness of God. At the same time, our faithful and loving God heals our heart and sets us free from personal strongholds."

* * *

Before becoming a Christian, I suffered from sleep paralysis and from ruminating, catastrophic thinking. I had a stronghold in my life. Some fiery trials dealt a crushing blow to the stronghold that was ruining my life, which at the time I was completely blind to.

Back in my heathen days, I did not believe in the occult. To control my world, I went into "the power of the mind"—a theosophy mentality, the mind-science stuff. After coming to the Lord, I made a vow never to practice this stuff again. However, the temptation often came to implement these practices. It was a battle. I resisted with the word of God. I rebuked it in the name of Jesus: "I resist you in the name of Jesus. Get out of here!" I attained victory over it.

There are things that happen to us in life that set us up for strongholds in our minds. For me, though I found victory, there was a stronghold still messing with my mind as a believer in Christ. How about you?

I was born with a partial cleft palette. The back of my mouth opened into my sinus cavity. There was nothing there. No palatine uvula. The upper bone only covered less than half of the roof on my mouth.

As an infant, eating was dangerous for me. In order to survive, I had to have reconstructive surgery, and not just one. I went back for several surgeries. I was a little tyke, around two or three years old. My earliest memory is of one particular surgery. I recall the event with such accuracy, my mother asked me how I even remembered.

Things were different back then. I was put on a gurney. People wearing white held me down and strapped me to it and then wheeled me down a sterile hallway. I was stripped away from my mom and dad and all the time screaming for them.

I could not talk and had no way to enunciate words even if I could. Little kids have no understanding of what is going on when things like this happen. I simply recalled my parents fading in the distance while being wheeled down a cold hospital hall. I was crying and terrified.

Then, the room. Someone placed a device over my nose and mouth—the smell of ether. I was a toddler. Can you imagine?

When I woke up in a room, things were stuffed into my mouth. Strange people came and went. I was strapped to the bed, unable to move to keep me from pulling the stuff out of my mouth and flailing about.

I was just a tyke and my parents were gone. Imagine the terror of it all! Little kids cannot process such trauma. Since I couldn't eat food with my mouth, I was fed by a tube. I was strapped down and scared spitless. I never realized the surgery saved my life because the trauma erased all of that.

Fortunately, the Lord had an older lady sharing the room in a bed next to mine. Years later, my mom told me that the lady was recovering from gallbladder surgery. This was the early 1960s. Things were done differently than they are today.

I have a vague memory of this woman singing to me. This woman sang and calmed me down. (I attribute my desire to play the trumpet and the guitar to her singing.) God put this Christian lady, whom I did not know, in the same room next to me.

Back then, parents were not allowed to stay overnight. They were only allowed a few hours of the day for visitation. Every time my parents departed, I panicked and cried. This trauma implanted a vast stronghold in my life. Though I recalled the incident, I never thought it had any effect on my life, but it did.

Being strapped to the gurney and wheeled down the hall, I wanted my mom and dad to rescue me. "Pay attention! Do you hear me? Do you see me? Help! Where are you? Why?"

I never saw this. Never realized the implications and the effect it played out in my life. Through constant failures, I played the blame game, never realizing I was my own problem. That is, until the Lord revealed it to me.

God gets through to you. After all, He is faithful to perform His word, *"that they may have life, and that they may have it more abundantly"* (John 10:10 NKJV). He healed my shattered heart that this ordeal caused.

Strongholds need to be dealt with before you become one of God's trees of righteousness that provide comforting shade for those around you. If not, you will hurt others and press your demands and needs onto those around you. Your insecurities and demands and control on others will not draw people to you but repel them from you. Churches are filled with members and even leaders like this.

This fortress came into being in my life back then. The devil does not play fair. He used it to his advantage, all because as a kid I was traumatized when I was stripped away from my parents.

You see, from the trauma I had the need to maintain control so I could be in charge of my world. No one was going to strap me down. Yet my life always had the rug pulled out from under me. That was my stronghold. What about yours?

So I dabbled in the mind-science cult. I did so without thinking it had any occult overtones. It was the power of the mind I could use so I would never be forsaken again!

Although I didn't know it then, that mind-science stuff is *definitely* demonic. I didn't even realize it. My walls of pride and determination grew stronger around me. I was determined not to lose control again. How about some of you?

This stronghold needed to come crashing down. As a Christian, I came to terms with the mind-science occult stuff and stopped it. Yet problems continued. The effects of trauma forced me to refuse to let people go. I ruined many relationships and friendships because of that. I drove people away from me. I was blind to it all until Jesus revealed it to me. As a friend of mine would say, "Oh, what a thought, praise the Lord, glory hallelujah!" He set me free. The stronghold came crashing down. Free at last—free at last!

Everyone is different. Your stronghold may differ from mine. This may require you walk alone so you discover how Jesus is always with you. How else can you learn love?

He was with me when I was a child. The lady who sang to me proved that. No matter what it takes, the Lord will get you through it. He is the ever-faithful God!

What the devil used to wreck my life, God turned it around for His greater good. He healed my soul, mended my broken heart. I am no longer held in bondage to "Don't leave me! Don't go!" I am free from rejection and the need to be seen and heard! My pride was dealt a needed blow and kept in check with continual pruning.

What the devil meant for evil, God turned to good. Let me pray for all whose strongholds have you down:

> *Heavenly Father, in Jesus' name I ask on behalf of those so bound and held captive that they would become totally free from their strongholds.*
>
> *If there is something in their heart that caused their wounds, that caused them to get into stuff they should not, I ask that You reveal to them the root cause of their stronghold. No matter the pain, pull out the splinters so only Your healing balm remains.*
>
> *In the name of Jesus, by the authority of the Lord Jesus Christ, as a believer that stronghold will come down by the power of the blood of Jesus. Any darkness inside will be revealed, and I ask You, Lord, to walk them the rest of*

the way so they can now provide shade to those in need of mending the way You mended them.

They will be set free in Jesus' name, no matter how painful or bad. Whatever it is, be removed in the name of Jesus. In the name of Jesus, I ask that these folks be set free according to Your promise to heal the broken heart, set the captive free, release them from what has them bound, open their blind eyes like You did mine. In Jesus' name, amen.

Think of it—the Lord of all glory prepared a place for us in heaven. Let that sink in. None of us deserve this honor. No, not one. Yet due to God being true to all that He is, He provided for us to be His own through Jesus' work on the cross, alone.

We will be involved in heaven, helping Him tend and take care of God's precious things. That brings Him great pleasure. We share in that. It's our inheritance as the "reconciled." We share this most effectively when our box of nails is removed, which often comes by the changing of many tires.

The fact that the Lord of glory has prepared such a place should make us grateful. The One we trust came and died in our place, paying our sin debt in full, proving Himself trustworthy and faithful. We can trust One who loves, reasons, and provides a choice when we had none. It is safe to surrender unconditionally to Him so you walk in the resurrection of new life. I was walking toward such a great inheritance.

It's true, God doesn't need any of us, yet He made us for the purpose of knowing Him as faithful and true. He never denies Himself in any manner. He is God Almighty, ever faithful.

One thing I learned over time is how God sovereignly weaves things together in this life in amazing ways. No matter how things swing, He remains faithful and will see us through. That is how we become His plantings, His trees, to help stop whatever lays waste to our lives and the lives of others. The simple answer is we become healed through our sufferings. He helps us recover by healing our broken hearts.

In many diverse ways, God works through life lessons, and from them He forms a sense of purpose and belonging. Fellowship blossoms between God and one another.

That's the secret—the faithfulness of God. He gets us through all life's storms. As the Bible says in 2 Corinthians 1:3-4, we comfort others by the same comfort we received from God. By this we become the plantings of the Lord so folks can rest in the shade He brought us.

God's character traits and nature define His faithfulness. He is unchanging in these. He will not deny Himself or who He is. We learn of His faithful character in the Bible.

For example, we find His character traits listed in Deuteronomy 32:3-4. More of these traits were revealed when the Lord passed by Moses in Exodus 34:1-9 declaring His name—His character traits. In Job 34:10-12, Elihu adds to the list. I can go on, but that is a good start to build true faith in Him. What do I mean?

In whom do you have your faith? We must put our faith in God and no other. Faith in ourself does not cut it. Our personal character traits let us down every time. I suggest you all do a little digging, a little Bible exercise. Go to Hebrews 11, and wherever you find the word *faith*, add this parenthetical: "in God's faithfulness." Oh my, how the Bible opens up our understanding big time.

Now faith [in God's faithfulness] *is the substance of things hoped for, the evidence of things not seen. For by it the elders obtained a good testimony* (Hebrews 11:1-2 NKJV).

But without faith [in God's faithfulness] it is impossible to please Him, for he who comes to God must believe that He is, and that He is a rewarder of those who diligently seek Him (Hebrews 11:6 NKJV).

No matter the box of nails tossed in our path, no matter the strongholds these cause, no matter what, the Lord gets us through it all.

It is easy to lose sight of God's faithfulness. Things happen in life that distort this truth and stop people from seeing the faithfulness of God. Strongholds.

The Bible teaches about strongholds in 2 Corinthians 10:4 (NKJV): "*The weapons of our warfare are not carnal but mighty in God for pulling down strongholds.*" We have strongholds, fortifications, set up within our minds that come about by the things we all go through in life, what we have done, or what others have done to us. These affect us in our relationship with Christ.

Some people live in one failed relationship after another. Others struggle with catastrophic thinking, blasphemous thoughts, or the need to control. There are many more.

The weapons of our warfare are not carnal but mighty in God for pulling down strongholds, casting down arguments and every high thing that exalts itself against the knowledge of God, bringing every thought into captivity (2 Corinthians 10:4-5 NKJV).

Ephesians 6:13-19 talks about the armor of God. If you're savvy enough, you will realize the armor is describing God's character traits. The armor is God Himself, how He is true to Himself and to His people.

God is a God of truth. He helps us walk in truth. This undergirds us and gives us strength and truth. Gird yourself with that truth of who Jesus is and His promise to deliver you by revealing the root cause that drives you to live in bondage.

The breastplate of righteousness is very important. As a new Christian you are the righteousness of Christ Jesus. You rely on the righteousness that Jesus imputes to you. The devil has no right to grab your heart anymore. You can say, "In the name of Jesus, get out of my heart." We must resist the devil.

Our faith is a shield against the enemy. All fiery darts are quenched because He is faithful and true.

The trials of life refine our faith and expose strongholds. The armor of God helps cast down arguments and all high things that come against the knowledge of God. He keeps His promises as John 15:1-8 points out.

CHAPTER EIGHTEEN

HEAVENLY COUNCIL

"He is the Rock, His work is perfect; for all His ways are justice, a God of truth and without injustice; righteous and upright is He."

—Deuteronomy 32:4 NKJV

Jesus and I came out of the forest and began walking in the rural countryside of gently rolling hills and fields spotted with trees and brush.

The colors of the trees and meadows in heaven are more pronounced than they are here. The colors you see in heaven cannot be seen with our naked eyes here on earth. Great beauty, joy, and light abound. We passed orchards whose trees were ripe with fruit. Since there is really no need to eat there, the fruit and grain were simply to enjoy. I recall a vineyard with big grapes. These were not for wine or drink. Looking back at this, from that day forward till now, I realize how these grapes are symbols for God's prophetic wrath to come at His appointed time, when humanity ultimately perverts, changes, and rejects all overtures to turn back to Him, clinging to the anti-Christ instead (Revelation 14:10).

(This is where my desire to look into biblical prophecy came from, teaching me to use logic and critical thinking, to examine the times and the hour in which we live.)

This vineyard's fruit reminds me of the urgency to examine the days in which we live and the fruit that grows more and more within me ever since. We need to prepare our hearts for what will fall upon the world by paying attention to the faithfulness of God, come what may.

The Bible marks the beginning of the end times with a falling away from the faith. The end times are marked by ever increasing evil and depravity. Meanwhile, the number of true believers become fewer and fewer so that only a remnant remains.

The end times are a time when the great merchants of the earth begin their dress rehearsals for developing what Revelation 13 describes. A time when we will see the spirit of antichrist growing stronger and stronger, forcing humanity to embrace the insanity of a new global world order.

Therefore, like the anti-Christ, the spirit of antichrist will mirror his characteristics in the world with ever increasing intensity as we near the last days. For example, Daniel 11:37 mentions how he will despise the desire of womanhood. Likewise, as we near the last days, that same attitude will be seen.

All things about womanhood, like giving birth, will be mocked by gaslighting people who believe that men can become pregnant, lactate, and give birth. Womanhood will be scorned so much that folks will not define what a woman is. Rather, womanhood will be maligned in every conceivable fashion in exchange for an androgynous complex to rule. Infanticide will be glorified as a right. The role of the family and parents will be destroyed.

The devil hates womanhood. For by woman, Jesus came into the world and defeated him soundly. So is it any wonder that in the days leading up to the last days such gaslighting will be justified and passed off as truth? That's why the truth and healing of Jesus Christ is needed. Scripture says, *"He sent His word and healed them, and delivered them from their destructions"* (Psalm 107:20 NKJV). Unless we know His Word, His Son, who is the source of all truth, we are left to the lies of the enemy and our destruction.

Daniel 11:23 mentions the lawless in the end times. One will come to power using great deceit through a small group of influential people. Before the end, freedoms will be denied. Soon we will see meetings proclaiming the need to track and monitor every human being. Their rationale: it's for our safety!

These are the great merchants, great men of the earth, the cream of the elites who gain control by stealth and gaslighting.

As Daniel 7:25 points out, the spirit of antichrist will be seen in the attempt to alter laws worldwide and even the seasons. Climate change (global warming) will be used to twist laws in a manner that enslaves people to the whims of the elite ruling class.

They will alter the reality of nature and time by redefining truth, morality, and social values by utilitarian means to control all. You'll hear those great men and merchants of the earth justify the need to alter human DNA for the noblest reasons but with the hidden intent of making humans compliant, subservient to them.

This small group of elitists thinks that they are better than others, that they can even become gods. Laws will be broken and altered with impunity by such people. It will be their way or the highway on a worldwide scale.

The stage for the lawless one to come into the world is being laid down. Since the real anti-Christ will war against the saints of God, likewise there will be a push to remove Judeo-Christian and the great Western traditions off the map.

True Christians must prepare their hearts in the faithfulness of God to endure and overcome till the blessed hope comes, just as Isaiah 26:19-21 and 1 Thessalonians 4:13-18 and 5:1-11 reveals.

Let our hands be fixed to the plow despite all the boxes of nails tossed along our personal crimson way. Let's be found working in God's field in many diverse ways both known and unknown helping to bring in the last harvest. Is this the great end-time revival?

What I do know is that such a revival is not what most think; rather, it is a curtain opening, exposing evil for what it is. The time before evil takes center stage in full is only a short seven years.

* * *

I recall how we passed the vineyard. By the curve of the road were bread ovens on the side of a gentle sloping hill. Various sized angelic beings were baking bread with some saints of God. I cannot tell you the reason why I saw this. It reminded me of the word of God, the bread of life that God has for His people. I can only imagine that this bread spiritually feeds the seeking heart during their prayer and Bible study time.

We walked along the narrow trail between two hills and more meadows toward a grand estate with too many rooms to count. Traveling there, we passed through areas like small villages as well as individual dwellings and storage areas, where people could stay and take care of the things of God. We entered a grand estate. I had no idea who it belonged to. Jesus was there, but I couldn't see Him. I looked around.

The structure of this place was indescribable, simply beyond words. Beautiful shades of blue and white emitted great peace.

Many chairs rose from the floor like blocks. When sat on, they perfectly conformed to you. There were other huge chairs where great angelic beings would sit.

Many folks and angels entered while others left. Stunning singing could be heard coming from outside. The ceiling was high above me, yet I knew there were many floors and rooms all around and above.

To me, this living area appeared as though prepared for rest and fellowship with others in a joyous, celebratory manner. It made an impression on me that reflects John 14 as a reality:

> *Do not let your heart be troubled; believe in God, believe also in Me. In My Father's house are many dwelling places; if it were not so, I would have told you; for I go to prepare a place for you. If I go and prepare a place for you, I will come again and receive you to Myself, that where I am, there you may be also. And you know the way where I am going* (John 14:1-4 NASB).

I did not know whom it belonged to. That intel was not granted to me. Rather, it was for me to observe and reiterate here that it is true, there are many rooms and dwellings God has for those who are in His beloved.

Heaven is a vast area. There are many abodes like this containing many rooms and dwellings. Each room or dwelling is uniquely prepared by Jesus.

Inside such rooms, you can find plants and outdoor scenery like a botanical garden. This old world is not our home—heaven is. I left this grand estate with a Bible verse resonating inside me:

> *But as it is written: "Eye has not seen, nor ear heard, nor have entered into the heart of man the things*

which God has prepared for those who love Him"
(1 Corinthians 2:9 NKJV).

I found myself outside this estate walking toward Jesus. He was speaking to others under a garden-like gate lined with beautiful green hedges. The hedges arched over the top held up by stunning latticework forming a garden passageway. Flowers lined the walkway. The peace here surpassed all understanding. Birds chirped. That great heavenly choir was singing off in the distance.

We followed this hedged pathway into the most astounding and unique area I ever saw. How I got to this spot, I cannot explain. Jesus was ahead of me, moving quickly through a great crowd. However, His presence remained with me and filled this place. I could not step any further into this profound area other than to stand right on the border before a glorious scene.

Daniel 7:9-10 describes the same place. I call it the heavenly council room. I cannot tell you if it was inside a building or outside. It was beautiful and garden-like yet a great gathering hall. First Kings 22:19-28 describes this as a place where God includes those He created in carrying out His will and plans. He does not need to do this, but He does because He is the God of the living. I recall standing transfixed, drinking it all in. The greatest throng of angelic beings was gathered around as well as believers facing a brilliant light in the very far distance. There appeared to be four, but I could only see three great angelic beings whose wings covered this brilliant light.

From this area, many angels were sent out to do tasks according to the will and word of God they received. They went out of one of the twelve gates to carry out God's will or justice outside the gates while the saints inside stayed to pray. I was amazed and awed.

An extremely tall, well-built angelic being stood off to my side, standing at the very apex of this place with crossed arms. He had four faces, but all I could see was the face of a man. His skin was like bronze and he had a body like a man. His eyelids appeared to have slits in them that enabled him to watch all things at the same time.

The praising and singing was beautiful and ethereal. Then, as though on cue, I turned and stepped out of the area and found myself walking in the countryside further into heaven's glorious land.

CHAPTER NINETEEN

WHEN EVIL ENDS

"There is a river whose streams shall make glad the city of God, The holy place of the tabernacle of the Most High."
—Psalm 46:4 NKJV

How can you describe what you see in such a place as this? No words can adequately describe its ambience of love.

We seemed to be walking slowly but apparently were not. Time in heaven is different than on earth. The hills and dales, the scenery passed by quickly. People greeted Jesus and He them. Great joy and peace prevailed. Heaven is where one lives forever whole and sound in so great an inheritance purchased by the blood of Christ. All things become new. No deformity or loss exists there. The breeze was gentle, like the breath of God. It was invigorating and filled us with a deep respect and love for God.

We came to a rounded rise overlooking a broad river. In fact, Ezekiel 47:1-12 describes such a river flowing out from heaven. Various sizes of glorious trees lined its banks. Some were huge. One such tree in the far distance spanned its great width. Instinctively, I understood that its source came from the throne of God. Prophetically, at the end of the tribulation period, when Jesus physically returns to set up the Millennium reign of Christ on earth, this river will be manifested on earth. Its purpose is to heal the earth and the nations during the thousand-year reign of Jesus on earth when all the promises made to Israel will come to pass.

Before that time comes the seven-year tribulation. As God judged the gods (fallen watchers and demons) of ancient Egypt explained in Exodus 12:12, so will the entities Paul spoke of in Ephesians 6:12 be judged.

The works of these devils will finally be judged for all the deception, ruin, and pain they caused. Then these legions will be cast into the pit, that abyss, the current hell, along with the devil himself and all who reject Christ.

After one thousand years, only the devil is released from the abyss (see Revelation 20:1-3). He will have no angelic or demonic help to hide behind to use as scapegoats to escape God's final justice. All his spiritual minions will have been permanently sealed in hell.

After the devil is released, he will be exposed and judged and held accountable for creating rebellion and malice. He will be turned over into the lake of fire just as God decreed in Psalm 82:6-7 and Revelation 20:7-15.

Our Lord God is the faithful God. He is in all ways more than able to fulfill His word. God keeps His word and is faithful to perform it.

For now, He did not leave us as orphans to the devil's devices. We are reconciled as His representative authority on this earth. We are born again by the Holy Spirit and have authority to wage this cosmic spiritual war between good and evil (see Ephesians 6:12).

Think: Jesus proclaimed that out of our inner being shall flow rivers of living water. With such waters, the Holy Spirit heals a dry and thirsty land that has forgotten the refreshment and faithfulness of God.

What does it mean to dispense living water to a dry and thirsty land?

After sin entered the world through Adam, we became spiritually dry, parched, and taken captive to do the devil's will (see 2 Corinthians 4:4). Revelation 12:3-4 reveals how he sent his minions to enforce his will of absolute authoritarianism over humankind to achieve a more well-ordered, controlled world.

This is seen in ancient history through kings, emperors, great merchants, and the intellectual elite worshiping these beings as gods. In turn, these devils helped maintain control over the masses for profit, and even nowadays their antics inspire many political philosophies and ideologies seen today.

It is a great error to assume these entities don't exist or to limit what happened in Genesis 6 as only concerning the human agents from the sons of Seth and daughters of Cain. "The sons of God" refer to the fallen watchers or angels, angels that modified human DNA to create a new type of human called Nephilim!

Think of it: due to the fall of humanity we have a sin nature. As human beings we are naturally rebellious. If the devil takes over, humanity will rebel even against him. To thwart this, as well as to stop God's redemptive plan, humanity was altered to make human beings compliant slaves and playthings for evil's amusement.

Jesus warned us in the scriptures that the last days will be like the days of Noah and Lot. We are seeing the governing elites today pushing to modify human DNA in order to make designer babies, to blend humanity with computers—to make trans-human beings who are easily tracked, monitored, and controlled to comply to their authoritarianism (see Ecclesiastes 3:15).

All this is out in the open, easily researched in their own papers, websites, and research. Some things do not change, when humanity only listens to a cunning serpent in a tree.

* * *

"Yep, some things just don't change," answered Night Ryder. "Not at all."

Tina: "The Bible, in Ecclesiastes 3:15, tells us plainly that what happens in the past repeats itself in various ways. Patterns seen in history repeat themselves and, finally, God will require an accounting from both humanity and the fallen angelic world."

"Yep, that's right, Tina and Night Ryder! We see this in both the books of Genesis 6 and Revelation. These boxes of nails, the fallen watchers cast to the earth by the great dragon's tail, taught humanity to live a new way and became known as gods to the ancient world."

> *The Nephilim were on the earth in those days, and also afterward, when the sons of God came in to the daughters of men, and they bore children to them. Those were the mighty men who were of old, men of renown. Then the Lord saw that the wickedness of man was great on the earth, and that every intent of the thoughts of his heart was only evil continually* (Genesis 6:4-5 NASB).

"In fact, the storylines of these ancient pagan gods reveal how they groomed humanity to act as they do to work their knowledge of what is good and what is evil to make their own version of paradise. Who needs God?"

Tina chimed in, "Yes, both Adam and Eve bought that lie in the Garden. The fruit of such knowledge looked like good, fresh bread that enlightened the eyes and made one wise enough to carry out schemes to make a new, better, more perfect world."

"Wow, Tina, that's good! Maybe that 'Build Back Better' slogan mirrors this too," Ryder jokingly quipped.

"I agree with you both. This is what is sold to the world's political and elitist class to make a better world in which they work the knowledge of good and evil to their own advantage to make their version of utopia on earth a reality. These fallen angels, watchers, pagan gods want folks to act like they do in their storyline."

Ryder responded, "Makes sense to me. Do you have any insight from your heaven experience on how the fallen watchers were able to gaslight humanity into thinking and acting like they do?"

"Yes," I replied, "but it has taken years to unpack."

* * *

You could say these entities were the superheroes of their day whom their human followers would emulate. Thus, the pagan gods (fallen watchers, demons) were viewed as "go to" agents to attain what one needed to make a better world for themselves. In fact, the storylines of the old pagan gods, those fallen watchers, espouse sexual perversion. Or they claim one can achieve a better world by escaping into drugs, alcohol, living a life of revelry, a "do as thou wilt" life. Some are lewd, sow contentiousness, or display outbursts of wrath, hatred, and ruthlessness.

There is, however, a price to pay to gain and maintain great power. Some involved the fires of Molech—infanticide to maintain the deal. That same storyline teaches humanity this same construct today. We see deviancy going after kindergarteners up to 12th grade to justify how cool it is to transition in order to be liked, accepted, admired. These entities teach that one can get what they want through conjuring and by methods of divination mentioned in Ezekiel 13:17-23. They are enchanters, enticing with beauty, greed, jealousy, envy, mind games, and even by killing certain people before their time to achieve a personal paradise.

Thus, entire populations are initiated to accept all manner of perversities God hates, but which they justify as the means for transforming the existing world into a better world. These ancient concepts are breaking forth again today. So one must do what God hates—that is the "noble good." Be free, do as thou wilt. Tear down walls. Destroy the old order as the best way to achieve a new reality, a utopia (see Revelation 12:1-6; Genesis 6:1-7; Proverbs 6:16-19). In the days of Noah (see Genesis 6:1-7), these fallen entities came to set up humanity to tempt God to destroy all humanity and to prove that He cannot fulfill His callings found in Genesis 1:1-26-29 and 2:15.

* * *

"Wow, this makes me think, Bryan, of a question that many have about the tree of knowledge of good and evil. Why did God place such a tree in the Garden in the first place?" queried Tina.

"Well Tina," I said, "the devil is caught in a snare, found in a tree. God's justice prevails, which proves to all how the old devil works good and evil to produce a living hell within this arena called earth."

CHAPTER TWENTY

SNARED BY A TREE

"Now the serpent was more cunning than any beast of the field."

—Genesis 3:1 NKJV

Overlooking this mighty heavenly river, the river of life, I could see many tributaries flowing from it out into heaven's vast interior. The trees along it were grand and beautiful to behold. Ezekiel describes a great tree extending over the river's width. There are things you come away with from an experience like this that you have trouble expressing. It takes time to digest what you learn. For example, why would God allow His angels to rebel against Him, His order, design, and ways? But praise the Lord for stopping Adam and Eve from partaking of the tree of life in a fallen state! Mercy comes in many shades.

It is true, as I learned from seeing hell—before perfection can come, one must first remove dross. God had a plan, sealed by the Lamb of God slain before the foundation of the world, to bring about God's perfection where there would be no more sin, death, or rebellion again (see Revelation 21–22).

God is absolutely just in all His ways and will not pervert justice, just as Job 34:12 reveals. The Lord cannot deny Himself or who He is. He is loving, merciful, kind, showing great grace, patience, and justice in how He holds the guilty to account.

How? God lives true to Himself. After all, God is all powerful and all knowing, so what does He have to fear? He is God who tests the heart and mind just as Jeremiah 17:10 reveals. He tests. That is a biblical principle. He granted His angelic beings moral reasoning. One third rebelled and the other two thirds remained loyal. He found what was in their hearts. Why would God test? The short answer is He is just in all His ways, even toward those angelic beings He created with intelligence to act responsibly with reason, but instead they chose to rebel thinking they could get away with it.

For example, the angelic ringleader of rebellion—as Ezekiel 28:11-19 states, iniquity was *found* in his heart, not *placed* in his heart. To place it would cause God to violate His own character and nature in the fullest sense of being just, even to one who before rebelling was endowed with gifts of life, reason, and intelligence.

God reneges on no gift or calling as Romans 11:29 declares. Even if foreknowing that some would make dross out of His creation. God is true to His nature that He can be trusted and He is faithful and true. But to just whisk these off into nonexistence would cause the Lord to cease to be the living God—the God of the living. He would be in violation of the gift of life He gave by taking it away (see 2 Samuel 14:14; Ecclesiastes 3:11,14).

Thus, an eternal, never-ending hell was made for such who rebel (see Matthew 25:41). Because to be absolutely just also means God will not let those sentenced forever as guilty, get off the hook. God foresaw all this. Hell awaits.

Truly He can shape (fashion) evil to bring about good, as Isaiah 45:5-8 proves, by using the dark threads of providence so His redemptive thread finally remains secure. His wisdom is greater than ours. God is more than able to work all things together for His good and reach His final goal by the Lamb of God slain before the foundation of the world.

Therefore, enter the creation of Man, Adam and Eve, where God triumphs. There He never violates or denies who He is and what He is like.

The fallen angels reasoned they could work the knowledge of good and evil to their advantage by pitting God's character traits and attributes against each other. Prove God can't live up to His own standards by their continual changes. Thus, the stage was set for a new heaven and earth to come after the final purging of the dross. This started when the devil was ensnared in a tree, revealing how he sells his wares so the results will be well seen on earth. God proves to all how merciful, good, and willing to forgive He is. Before the perfect can come, one must first begin to remove the dross. Dross is slowly revealed by the heat of the fire where it is scooped out so that finally only purity remains.

* * *

Tina interrupted, "So what you're getting at is that by the fall of man, the devil tried to get God to violate His word spoken to humanity found in God's promises in Genesis 1:26-31 and Genesis 2:15?"

"Yes," I replied. "That's how the old devil works in this cosmic war of good versus evil. The devil use humanity in an insane attempt to prove to God Himself that He cannot perform His own word and thus cannot keep His promises."

"Wow, I get it," said Night Ryder. "God gave us a free moral will. I see in those verses in Genesis you mentioned that Adam and Eve were to name the animals, be in charge of this earth, and tend and keep the Garden of Eden. Likewise, angels were granted free will so they could exercise their assignments in heaven. If they were not designed with free will, then God would be unjust as their creator. He is just first to Himself, proven in all things He does."

Tina interjected, "If God is not true to all that He is, then the devil could indict God as a divine puppet master who never gave anyone a chance. I see that."

"Let me say something here," I replied. "In Ezekiel 28:11-19 we see that the devil's iniquity was found in his heart, not placed there. In Isaiah 14:12-15, it tells us that he said in his heart that he wanted to exalt his throne above God's. Finally, Revelation 12:1-4 and 7-10 mentions there was a rebellion in heaven and a war as well. All this points out that free moral will was granted to all God's created angelic host. Does this mean He is a slave to it? No, God is not a slave to free will.

"In fact, He proves His omnipotence and sovereignty true by being true to Himself—by being able to work through all those He allowed to have a free will in ways beyond what we here on earth can fully perceive. However, in heaven things like this are made known."

"Yes, I'm beginning to see something here," said Tina. "It is like the fallen angels failed some sort of test. I see that in Ezekiel 28:11-19 and the other verses you mentioned. In fact, Psalm 7:9 mentions that God tests the heart. In Psalm 79:18, it tells of the children of Israel putting God to test. Likewise, rebellion puts God to the test by tempting God to go against His own nature and character."

"The devil and his angelic minions did so," Night Ryder said. "They tested, no, tempted God by playing God's good nature against Himself. The children of Israel did this too, as seen in Psalm 79:18. Knowing that God promised to care for them, they wanted food their way, not God's way. Amazing!"

"Yes, God's nature tests the heart to see if those He granted free moral will use it responsibly or abuse it. It is true, the word of God reveals the intents of the heart." I continued, "Thus, He teaches people what right and wrong is and justly removes the dross of rebellion and sin in the process."

"So in a sovereign, divine sense," Night Ryder replied, "God foresaw the need to remove the dross before the new heaven and earth can come. Wow, I see it now."

"Bryan," Tina asked, "I know others listening have the same question, but I have to ask for them—couldn't fallen angels be redeemed?"

"The answer is no; they cannot be redeemed."

"Why is that, Bryan?"

"Eternity, or one's eternal state, seals you. These beings were created as spiritual, eternal beings. What God foresaw in the heart of each needed to be dealt with so that His creation can be made absolute and justly free from all sin, iniquity, and rebellion as mentioned in Revelation 21 and 22. There is no injustice with God.

"What we can piece together from the Bible is that there is no redemption for the fallen angels. One reason is because they know too much about God's character traits. They were tested and found that they would continually exploit these in the vain pipe dream that they could trip up God. That cannot happen.

"There is a biblical principle found in 2 Chronicles 36:16: a time when there is no remedy. In other words, there comes a time when enough is enough" (see Revelation 19–22; Matthew 25:41,46).

"So with these fallen angels and demons comes a time without remedy. I wish He would do it faster," said Tina.

"I do too, Tina and Ryder. We need to remember these fallen spiritual beings were gifted with living eternally with intelligence and reason. They cannot die in the sense of going into a non-existent state. God justly made a place of punishment for them at an appointed time."

"So, Bryan, do you think God is collecting evidence in this life to send them there? What's your opinion on this?"

"Well, for starters, to finalize such a sentence involves collecting evidence to issue a final verdict of punishment for them. After all, God reneges on no gift, calling, or promise He decrees. They are proven, their hearts made known, by how they treated God and His gifts with utter contempt. There will be witnesses gathered to testify at an appointed time, just as Daniel 7 points out.

"God is thorough. Yes, He could have just wiped their clock clean in the very beginning due to His foreknowing of all things, but God had a plan—a just plan—way beyond what our minds can fully fathom.

"In this God proves Himself true in all that He is. In the process, those faithful to Him will see how great He is and worthy to be praised for all that He is—ever so true to Himself.

"As for us, God, foreseeing the fall of humanity, designed us with the ability for our mortal nature to die once. By this redemptive act, He saves those who heed His call from the second death to come.

"This proves His mercy and grace true to all in the process. The forever faithful and true God is worthy to be praised. We can trust Him completely. Look what He has done for us without our conditions getting in the way. He makes all things new, restoring us back to what He originally intended us to be."

"I see what you are getting at. It's mind-boggling, you all," Tina answered.

"Yes, it is," I replied. "Man was made lower than the angels—mortal!"

"I get it," said Ryder. "First death is when we die on earth and a second death for the unsaved after the Great White Throne Judgment verdicts are decreed."

"The saved don't face that second death but are reconciled and restored so they can live according to God's original plan and design in the new heavens and earth—entering into what God originally intended."

CHAPTER TWENTY-ONE

SPLASH A LITTLE WATER

"That you may walk worthy of the Lord, fully pleasing Him, being fruitful in every good work and increasing in the knowledge of God."

—Colossians 1:10 NKJV

We walked down the hill toward a glistening stream. Its waters were indescribable. This was just one of many tributaries flowing out from the river of life into this vast heavenly land.

In the future, these bring healing. For now, in this life, the healing waters from heaven come by the indwelling Holy Spirit of God gushing forth from us by the power of the Holy Spirit dispensed to those who come to freely drink living water (see John 7:37-38). Maybe we are to gush forth living water to the outcasts seen gathering around the wells mentioned in John 4:1-45?

I recall following Jesus along a path that led to the stream that flowed out from the river. The trees and lush land were filled with life. There were people and angels along the shore of the stream as we neared. Its width I would guess to be around

30 feet or so as streams go. Its water was of a quality I had never seen on earth. Its purity was supreme. We passed people swimming in its beauty. Great joy and loving happiness filled the air.

We came to a spot and stopped; children were playing in the stream. Jesus went into the water from about ankle to knee deep. He laughed. This was the Lord of glory, and the one like the Son of Man. Kids were splashing water on Him, and He did so in return.

He looked at me standing on the shore and smiled and said, "Ready," and they all began to splash water on me. I got into the river and splashed water on the laughing children, and Jesus splashed water on me—sharing joyous laughter the entire time!

At that point my trauma from seeing hell began to heal. I had PTSD but did not know it at the time as I kept so much bottled up inside. I wrote lyrics about this, but don't ask me to sing it because I can't sing very well.

Splash a Little Water

Come to the river of life my friends
Leave all your frown'n behind
Let's all run and jump right in
(Let me) splash a little water all over you
Heaven is not just a dream away
It is here before you now
Let's all dance along its shores
(Let me) splash a little water all over you
Hey, you drown'n in your all your tears
I see you're all sad and blue
Come run with me to the river's shore
(Let me) splash water—all over you

Hey, I keep a knock'n on your (front) door
Come on wake up you, sleepyhead
Let's go outside and play today
(Let me) splash water—all over you
How come you're always want'n stuff?
Did you forget I gave you abundant life?
Have you forgotten how to smile?
(Let me) splash a little water all over you
Didn't I promise living waters
To gush forth from your heart?
Come rebuild with me a new way
(Let me) splash a little water all over you
When I return to earth
Will I find any faith at all?
Wake up—time to get going
(I'm a) kicking water—all over you
Without any pain there can be no change
Hey, where's that cup of water?
Come on now—it's time to arise
(I'm a) kick'n water—all over you

How can I explain it? What happened at the stream began a process that slowly put my shattered life back together. Here the Lord of glory, who heals broken hearts, began with mine.

The time at this extraordinary stream remains etched in my memory. Much of it is too personal to explain other than laughter, great joy, peace that surpasses understanding.

For a brief moment, I understood what it means to be a human being created in the image and likeness of God just as He intended. I understood that it meant to reflect the attributes of His goodness, grace, mercy, righteousness on this earth by governing in that manner as His representatives. Jesus came, offering living water so we can learn to become, in this life, what it really means to be human, just as He originally intended.

In Genesis 1:26-28, God gave us His word to exercise dominion. This dominion was left to us to exercise with intelligence and reason. These are gifts from God who never reneges on the gifts, callings, or promises He gives. He is faithful to carry out His words and promises. He performs and keeps His word just as Isaiah 55:11-13 says. The dominion He gave us is not how we define it today but rather for reflecting the fruit of the Holy Spirit, which is love, joy, peace, patience, kindness, goodness, faithfulness, gentleness, self-control, righteousness, and truth (see Galatians 5:22-23; Ephesians 5:9-10). People often ask, "Why doesn't God just be God and stop all the corruption and evil?"

The answer is simple—He did by the Lamb of God, slain before the foundation of the world. For the Lord to stop evil in us means that He would need to do away with us. It is we who do evil and vileness and then pass laws to justify our actions. God gave His word to us in Genesis 1:26-28. The Bible has much to say about our authority as a believer, but human pride enters in and corrupts our exercise of dominion. The Lord of glory chastises us in order to expose and remove our pride. We learn that our sole source *is* from and in Him alone. Then true dominion is retained, and all is governed by the fruit of the Holy Spirit growing in our lives.

God keeps His word. He certainly performed it through what Jesus did upon the cross, which exposes and makes a public spectacle out of evil, condemning it justly in ways far beyond what our minds can fully grasp.

At an appointed time, all evil will be done away with, and the devil and his minions will be no more. All these will be confined in the lake of fire for eternity, reaping what they have sown. Humanity was originally made to reflect God's character traits on earth. That is what it means to be made/fashioned in His image and likeness. We are not to be little "gods." Instead, we are to govern the world with the fruit of the Holy Spirit. In this life, as His redeemed, we learn how to do this. The Bible tells us to love each other, be wise, know God, act in a right manner, show mercy and grace and goodness, live by truth. All these characteristics are attributes of God's character.

God so loved the world. He tends to it and keeps it. His love seeks what is lost. However, many love darkness more than His light. The word of God exposes this.

When we come to His light, we learn to shine forth the attributes of His great character traits of goodness and righteousness on earth. Oh, what a place this would be if we learned to govern our lives by His light! This life prepares us for the one to come.

* * *

At the stream everyone laughed and splashed. Jesus spoke with healing joy. The water was refreshing, reviving my soul and heart. The children happily frolicked and played. We left the stream. Jesus held the hand of a little one while carrying another on His arm; the others played and skipped along as we walked through the fields of heaven.

Soon, in a most gentle manner, several angels came for the kids. For some of these little ones, it was time to head back to that grand field of reunion and meet their parents. Oh, the joy that awaits!

My prior Christian concept of Jesus was rather stiff, distant. At least that is how movies portrayed Him and what most churches led you to believe back in the mid-1980s. Yet here in heaven, I saw Him as the Lord of glory, full of life, kindness, goodness, power, and authority too. As I read the gospel accounts of Jesus, I can imagine that when He walked this earth He was full of life and compassion and authority, all well balanced together.

Here we approached the crest, a small hill overlooking the landscape, fields, and the stream. We saw that everything was so filled with life. In this world, we see grand scenes of nature, but it is austere if you try to survive in its rawness alone for years on end. In heaven, it is not like that; it is full of life, so much so that human words cannot do justice in describing the beauty and ambience that is there. Walking the fields of heaven. Feeling the grass beneath my feet. Looking at all the trees, flowers, and, yes, animals that are there—it was amazing.

The time I spent at the stream began a process that slowly changed my life. This change happened slowly after my born-again experience that the began summer of 1980. Now, here, it took a new turn in learning to walk according to God's sanctifying crimson way.

Yes, I have had hard times, bad and good times. What I learned at the stream is lasting. It is in me, and I can't shake it no matter what comes. I know now for certain that my times are in His hands. I found rest and peace with God.

Don't get me wrong—this change came slowly, but I can trace it to the water from the stream, where it began to bathe my crushed spirit, wounded in this mortal life. Here my broken heart began to be mended. I had to learn to walk with the Lord who helped set me free from what held me captive and in bondage.

In this life, I learned how His words soothed and chastised me with the purpose to reveal what needs to be dealt with what is in my heart. From this, I discovered freedom from the prison of my bad thought patterns and attitudes. Most of all, the post-traumatic stress about seeing hell was dealt a final blow. Yes, I still have a few dreams. Yes, sights and sounds can still trigger memories, but the anguish is gone. I am no longer driven by it.

In other words, from the moment of splashing in the stream till now and beyond till I go home to be with Jesus, He uncovers the things that I used to justify living stupidly. These must go. I am no one great, and I still mess up. God's grace indeed changes me (see Titus 2:11-15; 1 John 1:9).

At times, these changes come with pain, like removing a festering splinter. But after their removal, healing begins just as Isaiah 61:1-4 says. That's what the healing waters from the river of life did for me.

Do you need this water? Healing from the trauma of this mortal life?

No wonder the woman at the well, mentioned in John 4, left her earthen water vessel at the feet of Jesus and ran to tell others of the One sent to rescue us. The whole town came forth to hear Jesus. They invited Him to stay. Will you?

I find from time to time someone with all brains and little heart trying to say that things like this just can't happen. All I can say is if that is you, may Jesus just splash a little water all over you.

CHAPTER TWENTY-TWO
HAY, WOOD, AND STUBBLE

"According to the grace of God which was given to me, as a wise master builder I have laid the foundation, and another builds on it. But let each one take heed how he builds on it."
—1 Corinthians 3:10 NKJV

Arriving atop an ascending rise overlooking heaven's vast landscape, it was as though heaven was shouting forth the faithfulness of God. Then we began to move down the spine of the crest through fields, past buildings and grand estates. I saw patches of woodland here and there and mountains in the distance. Angelic beings moved through the sky. No matter how one travels in heaven to a certain place, those heading there all arrive at the same time.

Walking with Jesus here, I learned something that has taken a long time to get through my thick skull. Jesus keeps His word. He is faithful to perform it, carry it out. However, it's not always the way we think He should. God is the faithful God!

Walking in the fields of heaven taught me things that have taken years to just begin to grasp. After all, it's part of uncovering a matter. It takes time, a journey. I ask, what is He teaching you in the here and now?

Jesus stopped, smiled. He did not need to say a thing. This was a beautiful place. The stream came back in view as it meandered around the hill. Along its banks I saw a man fishing. He waved. I did not think too much about this at the time as everybody who greeted Jesus knew Him in ways we can't fully comprehend here in this mortal life.

At the time I did not grasp why Jesus was showing me this particular place in heaven, but in hindsight I see it has to do with what theologians call the doctrine of rewards.

I do not fully comprehend the Judgment Seat of Christ by which our dross is removed and after that what our rewards will be. I do not think anyone really knows for certain. One thing that has stuck with me about this place is that our reward somehow concerns our position and role in the current heaven, as well as the future new heavens and earth to come. It is all in God's time, not ours. Our reward is an inheritance, incorruptible and undefiled, reserved in heaven for us just as 1 Peter 1:4 says. I do not think anyone here on earth can describe our inheritance in heaven other than—it is heaven itself and Jesus Himself. I fail miserably trying to explain it. What awed me about this location, which has taken years of studying the Bible to figure out, is that the Lord makes for His people their own special place. The Lord God is faithful. Jesus said He went away to prepare a place for us. He keeps His word.

This world is not our home. In this life we have toils, sadness, trials, travail, joy, happiness, good things, and blessings too. No matter what comes our way, bad or good, Jesus prepared a place for us who trust Him. He is faithful. We have His word on this. I suggest you read 1 Peter 1:3-12 soon as it reveals much of what I am trying to say here.

Keep this before you—this world is not our home. The One who promised is faithful to complete it. By it we will gain courage and overcome no matter the hardships or blessings that come our way.

Drinking in the scenery, my attention was drawn to the man seen in the distance fishing in the stream. Does that mean there are fish in heaven? Laugh all you want at this, but it just might be catch and release there! All kidding aside, for years I conjectured who this person fishing could be and why.

Years later, around 2016 or 2017, before my aunt passed away, she had her daughter send me a photo of my grandfather who passed away around 1964. My grandfather was born in 1877. He was an austere man, a disciplinarian, and a fiery old school Methodist preacher. My last memory of him was on his deathbed at an old soldier's home. I was told that he was a veteran of the Spanish-American War. He was being fed peas by a nurse. He saw me and pulled me close and began to pray over me with force while spitting chewed peas at me. I was scared to death. His hand lay heavily on top of my head. I have no idea what he was saying as I was around five or six years old at the time.

I never knew him but I heard the stories. He was a good man but also had his ugly streak as my relatives mentioned to me. People born in 1877 were of a different generation and their disciplinary ways are difficult to fully grasp for the modern mind. At least, unlike today, they held evil in check from overpowering the land.

My grandfather hailed from Scotland and lived in California. He attended the Los Angeles Bible Institute when R.A.

Torrey was dean of the school. That is who taught him. Look up who R.A. Torrey hung out with— Dwight L. Moody.

From what I can gather, he was there in 1906 when Azusa Street occurred. That move was not limited to only Brother Seymour's church. It spread about a mile along a swath of downtown LA. It was one big ongoing outpouring. It affected Baptists, Methodists, Presbyterians, and Independents. They all set up meetings there.

It was not all about speaking in another language either. Both those who opposed and those who spoke in other tongues set up meetings along that stretch of road. Masses of people were saved, discipled, and then went out to save the lost. My grandfather was a part of that. What part, I do not know. It affected him to attend Los Angeles Bible Institute during its fledging days. He went out and preached to the First Nations people and then came to Tennessee and Virginia, where he met my grandmother.

As best I can figure, since he was old school and I was the first male child of his oldest son, my dad, he blessed me. I was terrified by the experience as he spoke over me with force and spat peas out with nurses grabbing at him trying to get him to let go. To the mind of a five-year-old, things like this leave an impression. It took me a long time to eat peas again.

The photo my cousin sent me was my grandfather at 30 years old. I only knew him as an old geezer, stern, one who spoke and devils fled. His mere presence would chase any away in a matter of nanoseconds. The stories I heard about his preaching style and his strictness were legendary. I was left with the impression of both fear and awe of him. I never saw what he looked like at 30 years old, but folks in heaven look around that age, all made perfect, with all their hay, wood, and stubble burned away.

Then I saw the photograph. That was the man fishing in heaven. He was a fisher of men no less. Now, it all made sense. It is the glory of God to conceal things and for us to search out these matters. He had his flaws but was still a man of God. He left all, even his first wife and family, to minister to the Modoc Nation First Nations people of the Northwest.

What I gathered from reading some of his letters and poems and stories from my relatives is that he went to the Nez Perce tribes, and then into the Dakotas to the Cheyenne Agency, which later became the Cheyenne River Reservation.

Then they went back east to Virginia and Johnson City, Tennessee, where he helped found the old Methodist church there. His name is on a plaque on that building. Our real last name is Methvn, but he changed it to Melvin, from what I can gather, because people never pronounced it right.

Years later, in 2010, I was in Mescalero, New Mexico, speaking in the Apache Nation in a tent set on a high school football field. I heard the Lord speak this simple word to me without fanfare or explanation. He said, "Go to the Northern tribes." My answer was yes before realizing what had just happened. (He does speak in a still quiet voice, you know. The Bible says so.)

I went back to Colorado. A few months later, I received a phone call to come up to the Cheyenne River Reservation to speak there. I had never heard of the place. It was in South Dakota—the Northern tribes! So from 2011 till the COVID shut down in 2020-21, I was blessed to minister to the Lakota people of both the Cheyenne River and Standing Rock Reservation. It just happened. God put it all together with so many other great Christian people as a team.

At the time, I recalled a poem my grandfather wrote about a barroom with swinging doors somewhere in the prairie lands of the Dakotas. It amused me as a kid when I read it and was reminded of the evil of drink and loose women behind swinging doors. I do not recall the name of the town because the poem is now lost, but I think it may have been "Isabel." Many years later, in 2011, I was on my way to where my grandfather preached. In fact, I have been in Isabel, South Dakota, many times getting gas and eating at the only restaurant there—a bar and grill.

The fisher of men fishing in a stream in heaven was my grandfather at 30 years old. Then I went where he once trod. I hope he did a great work there. Maybe somehow, I was an answer to his prayer that he blessed me with while spitting peas. Only God knows for certain. He truly works in mysterious ways.

I shake my head over the smugness of some who believe that Jesus and the little children can't be like I described. Our loyalty is to be in Jesus Christ alone, not some person or their opinions. Amazing how folks give more honor to men than to the Lord God Almighty. Their fidelity is to defend their personal, constructed theology.

But God's grace is stronger. They will one day see heaven; maybe ride a horse they say can't be there. All their wood, hay, and stubble will be burned up, like all of ours will be at the Judgment Seat of Christ, which prepares us for our place in His great inheritance (see 2 Corinthians 5:10). Guess we just might be seeing each other there. Amen!

What happened to the 1906 Azusa Street Revival? It began to fizzle out about three years later (1909) due to some whom we would term today as Pentecostal big shots. They turned the movement into a work of man to make themselves out to be something they were not, and internal strife ensued.

These folks brought division into the body of Christ by being proud about the revival phenomena that occurred there. Some wanted to control it and take center stage. I will not mention the names. Brother Seymour was kicked to the side of the road by many of these big shots. The revival that swept through that mile-long segment of LA died out by around 1912–1915. In my opinion, such folks stained the name of Christ by their pride and desire to control things, as well as by the bad theology they brought in to justify it all.

Thank God, He burns up all the hay, wood, and stubble we have before we arrive completely into heaven. Just think if He did not (see 1 Corinthians 3:10-16)!

CHAPTER TWENTY-THREE

WITH EYES OF FIRE

"His eyes were as a flame of fire."

—Revelation 1:14 KJV

Every day is a new day. No one can tell what each will bring. You may find yourself either entering heaven or headed in the opposite direction that Jesus warned about in Matthew 10:28. Our journey in this life tests us. It asks, "Where do you put your trust: in yourself, political leaders and ideologies, wokeness, social justice, religion, church. Or do you trust in Jesus alone?"

I recall plainly walking through this land with unquenchable joy. The knowledge of God was indeed vast and wide. His appearance was as brilliant light, and His eyes were pools of flaming fire. Most important, of course, was a heart filled with compassion. Tragically, many people within the church trivialize Him. For many, He is simply the means toward some end, and they miss knowing Him and having a minute-by-minute mindfulness of His presence. Folks ask me, "What was it like to walk with Him in heaven?" Walking with Jesus in heaven was very healing and freeing. My crushed soul was revived, and my broken heart was healed. His words were active and alive. His words divided my soul and spirit, bones and marrow (see Hebrews 4:12-13). His words are wise and discerning. He is the living Word. His words He speaks cut to the division of soul, spirt, joints, marrow. His word discerns the thoughts and intents of the heart (see Hebrews 4:12).

This is part of what is seen in His eyes of fire exposing who really owns our faith! Each word He speaks fills a vast warehouse of wisdom that gives understanding and deep knowledge. His words grant us, as the apostle Paul prayed in Colossians 1:9, to be filled with the knowledge of His will in all wisdom and spiritual understanding so we can live alive unto the Lord.

In heaven, you know who Jesus is. You respect and are awed by Him and even more so when you see Him with all the children there and watch His interactions with each person. This singular attention causes your heart to love Him more and more. All misconceptions about God are washed away.

His presence permeates the current heaven. He is everywhere, but with you at the same time. No words can explain this to the rational, linear mind. At first when you see Him high and lifted up, you are, like Isaiah, undone by the experience and very humbled. Then you see Him as a friend, more faithful than a brother, and you begin to grasp the wonders of His faithfulness.

How could I, long ago as a sinner, hate someone like this? That thought weighs heavily on me today. Yet He forgave me and rescued me from the miry pit I had dug for myself and others too. So undeserving, He forgave me. I owe Him my very life! Take me, I am Yours. I love You, dear Lord Jesus, amen! You captured my heart! Can you say that? *Has He captured your heart?*

Years later, in 2011, while on the Cheyenne River Reservation, South Dakota, on a cold, wintery, below-zero day at the Moreau River Sanctuary overlooking the river, I wrote these lyrics titled "Safe Harbor" that encapsulate what I am trying to say.

Safe Harbor

Early I beseech thee
Early I seek thee
With my whole heart (x2)
As I travel the wilderness way
I've found You captured my heart
When I stumble and fall, You're there
Lift'n me up, drying my tears
Guiding our way to Safe Harbor (x2)
Early I beseech thee
Early I seek thee
With an aching heart (x2)
Here midst travail and pain
You send forth Your healing light
Dispelling this darkness that's all around
Apply'n Your healing salve
Guiding our way to Safe Harbor (x2)
Early I beseech thee
Early I seek thee
With a longing heart (x2)
Here midst travail and pain
I've found You captured my heart
When I stumble and fall You're there
Apply'n Your healing salve
Guiding our way to Safe Harbor (x2)

Today what strikes me in the Bible is how God spoke as a close friend to Moses. He speaks to us as a friend also. He spoke to Moses face to face, or *panim* to *panim*—presence to presence. I can imagine that this helped Moses lead a rebellious people to the promised land (see Exodus 33:11). Moses bore the word of God.

Today, we who are born again by the Holy Spirit are to carry the word of the gospel far and wide to a rebellious people held captive by one greater than Pharaoh. In doing so, people will be able to see the light of God's faithfulness in a dark word. The fall robbed humanity of living in the presence of God. It ruined our relationship with God and each other. When Jesus was nailed to the cross for our sins, He said simply, "Father, forgive them, for they do not know what they do." In other words, He was saying, "I take their punishment upon Me, on their behalf, so they may see what they do to each other and Me." With that, the word of God gives us a choice when before we had none.

Jesus willingly took God's wrath in our place for what we do to each other and God. He did this, so undeserved, so we can always be in His presence by the indwelling Holy Spirit, forever. We can now learn to live each day face to face with God in the cool of the day as a friend—His adopted, His own. Amen.

Can you really ignore that kind of faithfulness displayed by so great a love calling you to come? "Return to Me!"

If there is anything I learned from my experience of seeing this glorious land, it is this: His council will stand! Why? God is the faithful God who performs His word just as Isaiah 55:11 and Isaiah 46:10 say. He keeps His word; His promises, gifts, and callings are without repentance. After all, He is a faithful God, always true to Himself and all that He is, with no shadow of turning. His counsel will stand, and He will perform His word. An example of this is in in 1 Kings 22:1-40 where the prophet Micaiah (which means "who is like God") revealed the counsel of God and how He is faithful.

Ahab was a wicked, deceptive, manipulating king of the northern tribes. He learned well from his wife Jezebel. God determined the time of his departure was at hand to face the judgment of God and an eternity in hell. Micaiah reveals how God's counsel works. He involved His angels in the process as seen in 1 Kings 22:19-23, saying, "Who will persuade Ahab to die in battle?"

The determined council of God proclaimed His word would be performed. Why did God involve His angels in carrying out His will?

Ahab was a master manipulator and deceiver. His plan was to involve the righteous King Jehoshaphat of Judah in an unholy alliance with an enemy that threatened both kingdoms by planning to have Jehoshaphat killed in battle.

Ahab's plan involved dressing Jehoshaphat in his armor (see 1 Kings 22:22-30). In this way, the enemy would kill the king of Judah while believing they killed Ahab. Ahab did this with the intent of taking over the southern kingdom of Judah in the process.

An angel came forth in the heavenly council and told the Lord that he was willing to come as a lying spirit to the prophets of Baal whom Ahab listened to. Then God's word would be fulfilled by an arrow—a fitting payback for a deceiver.

God keeps His word. He is faithful to perform His word. Even more amazing is that He involves us, today, in the counsel of His will. How so? By granting us His authority used in spiritual warfare. The church is called to stand tall against evil, not to hide and cower in silence so that evil prevails. The church pushes against the tide. All great moves of God push against the evil of the day.

The world's prophets of modern, secular baals and the fallen crowd are held in check (see Ephesians 6:12). Plans are thwarted by the arrows aimed by the word of God.

We learn the secret of not cowering in silence by walking in the cool of the day in sweet fellowship, getting to know God who is faithful and true (see Revelation 19:11; 22:6-7) in the secret place of the Most High—our prayer closet, intercession.

There is a payback coming for those who seek to control it all, for those who love darkness more than light. He is faithful—all opposition against God's justice will come to an end in due time. We are to be part of that plan. Sadly, for many, their own wisdom causes them to cower and remain silent amidst encroaching darkness.

Those who hear His word return to Him by turning away from error. He helps us exercise dominion correctly by helping us to govern our lives by the fruit of the Holy Spirit. This pushes back against darkness by not being afraid of the cost.

If they come against you and me, their evil is exposed. Those who seek to save their lives will lose them, and those who lose their lives for His sake will find them, as Matthew 16:25-28 says. Think about this a bit. God has His arrows ready, while calling all one last time to return.

His eyes were as a flame of fire (Revelation 19:12 KJV).

His eyes are like flames of fire meting out final justice. A frightening sight to behold for those who buried their talent in the sand (see Matthew 25:24-30). Amen.

CHAPTER TWENTY-FOUR

CITY OF PEACE

"For they that say such things declare plainly that they seek a country. ...But now they desire a better country, that is, an heavenly: wherefore God is not ashamed to be called their God: for he hath prepared for them a city."
—Hebrews 11:14,16 KJV

It was nearing time to leave. We began a walk toward the grand city that I had seen earlier in the distance. The journey there I keep to myself. I recall it yet cannot tell anyone about it as it consists of glorious scenery and imagery and matters I'm not able to utter.

The trail led us through another patch of woodland—a very special place to me. Great happiness and wholeness and soundness awaits me there upon my return. I recall people passing by. Love, peace—profound.

We traveled a distance toward a great city, yet it took no time to get there. Time as we know it does not matter in heaven; there is eternal time, as I call it.

The city had streets of paved translucent gold. I instinctively knew where every building was and what was inside each. These were huge structures. Others varied in size. The city had beautiful botanical gardens. One particular place was where the books and records were kept. Though we were not close to it, I could see it within my mind's eye. Some of the buildings reminded me of the best ancient architecture of Bible times, an ancient, classical style but more stunning and larger than one might imagine. Other building shapes were too difficult to explain. This glorious city was adorned with the rural outdoor beauty. We neared a grand meeting hall that was wide enough, but its length stretched on and on. We went inside.

There angelic beings and saints of God were preparing the place for a great feast to come at an appointed hour. Tables sat low to the ground. Those attending would be able to sit comfortably and recline. Cups, plates, bowls, and various utensils were being set up in what looked to me to be a great maroon-colored tablecloth with gold trim with a bit of green, which I never have seen before. Other tables stretched the width and length. Saints and angelic beings who had sewn the fabric were placing more tablecloths. Others brought in the bowls and tall, uniquely shaped vessels that held water or some sort of refreshment. Some were helping others to follow the design given to decorate with a keen eye for every detail. Everyone was happy and busy.

As we walked through the great length of this huge dining hall, various segments were in the process of being set up. Walls were decorated with beautiful artwork, paintings made by beloved brothers and sisters. Golden candlesticks and menorahs lined the walls, while others were placed on the rows of tables. I could imagine that those folks who have gone on before us who like to decorate, plan, and organize fit right in here doing what they love for the Lord!

Now, all this was years ago in our time. I can only imagine how much more prepared this reception hall has become. I was glimpsing inside the great wedding hall where the wedding supper of the Lamb of God, slain before the foundation of the world, risen from the dead, will be held.

What I came away with from experiencing this great hall is that God blesses all whom the devil persecutes and makes weep in the great cosmic war of good versus evil. God blesses by restoring us back to His original creation and purpose—His beloved children who trust in His faithfulness, signed, sealed, and delivered as His own.

After my heaven experience, I became more aware of the great cosmic war that seeks to disprove God's faithfulness, to disprove that He is truly faithful keeping His word and performing it.

Many never realize how faithful our God is and live a self-inflicted, persecuted life seeking solace in things that never satisfy. For example, He gave us biblical prophecy warning us of what was to come and the need to prepare. He warned us of the devil's methodologies and ways. Yet many in the modern church have drifted away from God's warnings and solutions to combat the devil's schemes. When trials and tribulations come in our personal lives or on a worldwide scale, people scarcely know what to do. As I said before, the devil seeks to overthrow God and exalt his throne and authority above God's.

In the book of Job, a great cosmic war between good and evil transpired. Evil sought to disqualify God's goodness. Job was living in a fallen world, and the devil was walking about seeking someone to devour, to prove to God Himself that He cannot keep His word to those who belong to Him.

God knows all things and knew what the serpent of old was up to by walking to and fro on the earth, considering God's good servant Job. The Lord of glory beat the devil to the punch by saying, "*Have you considered My servant Job, that there is none like him on the earth, a blameless and upright man, one who fears God and shuns evil?*" (Job 1:8 NKJV).

Many folks miss the impact of what is being said. The devil was considering Job in order to prove that God was unreliable and would not keep His promises, gifts, and callings given to mankind (see Genesis 1:26-31; 2:15). The Lord God declared that Job was blameless and upright, one who fears and respects God and shuns evil. The devil was defeated the very moment God spoke these words. After all, as Isaiah 55:11 states, God performs His word, even in ways we do not realize. How so? The devil was considering the heart of Job and our hearts as well in this great cosmic war. Why?

Jeremiah 17:9-10 helps answer this. Due to the fall of humanity, the heart is now deceptive, warped, wicked, always twisting things for one's advantage. Who can know it? Someone must show us what we are really like inside. Verse 10 reveals that God tests the heart to give to each person the fruit of their ways and doings. The devil was considering the heart of Job; God spoke of him being upright, blameless, shunning evil, fearing God. *Blameless* means moral integrity despite one's personal flaws, while *upright* means ethical, righteous.

The Bible teaches how God blesses the upright in heart despite their flaws. (The story of King David also proves this.) God blessed Job with protection, blessings, land, and prosperity because Job trusted in the faithfulness of God (and so did King David). In Job 1:9-11 (NKJV) the devil said:

> *Does Job fear God for nothing? Have You not made a hedge around him, around his household, and around all that he has on every side? You have blessed the work of his*

hands, and his possessions have increased in the land. But now, stretch out Your hand and touch all that he has, and he will surely curse You to Your face!

Notice God was not taken aback by the challenge. He already foresaw what would come before anything was created. He told the devil to go ahead, give it his best shot—but he could not take Job's life. *Whose hand was against Job, God's or the devil's?*

The devil reminded God of Job's fallen sin nature that was hidden in Job's heart. So in Job 2:1-7, he accused God of showing partiality to Job by blessing him despite his human sin nature.

It was tantamount to the devil saying to God, "Take away all that Job has. Take away Your gifts; then Job will curse You. His sin nature, You know. Then if You are just, you must be rid of Job due to that alone. But if You keep blessing him, then You are not impartial. If partial, that proves You are not true to Yourself and all that You are because You can't keep Your word, callings, gifts, and promises because iniquity resides in the heart of all humanity. My throne will be above Yours, You know."

This tactic is the mainstay employed in this great cosmic war against all persecuted by the devil, who is trying to portray God's word as unfaithful. The meaning of Job's name is telling. According to *Smith's Bible Dictionary* and *Hitchcock's Bible Names, Job* means "the persecuted who weeps."

God is smarter than that! He is faithful to perform His words spoken over Job. Job would later be transformed by the words God spoke. We see this in the last chapter when he was blessed with a double portion. Then Job's heart was made new.

Our hearts are made new by the Lord in the new birth (see John 3), and will be rejoiced over during the great day of the feast in the grand wedding hall when there shall be no more tears.

The devil inflicted Job with physical and mental suffering to get "the persecuted who weeps" to curse God (see Job 2:3), to prove to God Himself that He could not keep His word and was guilty of being partial.

If God destroyed humanity in an unjust manner, how could He remain God? If God revoked all His promises, gifts, and callings granted to humanity in Genesis 1:26-28 and 2:15, God would be reneging on His promises. This absolutely will not happen, folks! God is the faithful God and more than able to keep His word. No one can outplay or outsmart God, even when the persecuted weep. So I ask, whose hand was against Job—God's or the chief adversary's?

The Lord God Almighty is faithful and true. He is more than able to perform and keep His spoken word and promises (see Isaiah 55:11; 46:10; Jeremiah 1:12; Ezekiel 12:25-28). The Lord of glory does not renege on gifts and callings (see Romans 11:29), no matter how many folks claim He did. In the great hall, we enter that blessing in full. Oh, the rejoicing!

Paul wrote in 1 Timothy 2:5 that the mediator who came to stand in the gap for the persecuted is Jesus Christ. He pleaded with God for our forgiveness while hanging on a cross, "*Father, forgive them, for they do not know what they do*" (Luke 23:34 NKJV). Truly, God keeps His word and reneges on no gift or calling. He is faithful. He grants us our authority to be able to resist the devil despite our shortcomings. He empowers us to live in this sin-ravaged world system that persecutes the souls of men and women to weep in anguish, causing them to live life cursing God by seeking comfort in addictions, power trips, sexual perversions, immorality, anger, malice, and by every evil work.

If there is a messenger for him, a mediator, one among a thousand, to show man His uprightness, then He is gracious to him, and says, "Deliver him from going down to the Pit; I have found a ransom"; his flesh shall be young like a child's, he shall return to the days of his youth (Job 33:23-25 NKJV).

Jesus hung upon the cross, our Mediator of a new covenant, in essence saying, "I will take the punishment for their iniquity hidden in the heart and expose it so that they may live with Me after I arise from the dead."

He sets you free from what holds you captive and heals your broken heart. He sets at liberty those held in their personal prisons, feeling they cannot escape. He opens the eyes of spiritual blindness so that you can see the faithfulness of God!

God is the faithful God. You can trust in such faithfulness, God's love is proved true by our Mediator, Jesus Christ. He will change the course of your life. In this life, as the persecuted who weep, we learn to walk blameless, upright, respecting God by learning to live responsibly before Him, learning to hold fast to moral integrity because He spoke over us His words.

Through Jesus, the word of God (see John 1:1), we received the gift of righteousness (see Romans 5:17; 2 Corinthians 5:21). God declared us righteous. He gave His word and proved it on the cross. He is faithful to keep His word. He calls us His own. Think on this for a moment: Job received his reward after coming to his senses after seeing how just God is. He repented and was restored. In heaven we shall be restored in ways beyond what Job received in this mortal life.

I long to return to that great hall, made new and whole and sound, and bring as many friends with me as the Lord has me to bring. Come!

CHAPTER TWENTY-FIVE

HEAVEN BECKONS!

"Blessed is he whose transgression is forgiven, whose sin is covered. Blessed is the man to whom the Lord does not impute iniquity, and in whose spirit there is no deceit."
—Psalm 32:1-2 NKJV

This great dining hall was simply amazing. Tables were being set and readied for that great day that awaits the redeemed. No more being the persecuted on earth. No more sorrow, no more sickness, no more sin. All things will be made new just as the Bible tells us.

We exited the grand hall into the city of indescribable peace. This heavenly city of God is beautiful to behold. It is unlike any city here on earth. There were buildings of various shapes amidst a lush, well-manicured, garden-like landscape. The refracted light of gold and gemstones glistened on the streets. We departed from the city and traveled back to the field of reunion. There, the Lord had me look back toward the city in the distance. I saw a city being prepared for the time when the new heavens and earth are tied back to the will of God. A time when all sin and wickedness is done away with just as Revelation 21 and 22 reveal.

In my mind, I still can see the field of reunion, as I call it, as plain as day. People meeting loved ones who departed before them. Off they went into the interior of the current heaven, joyous and healed. The laughter of children, the smiles and facial expressions of Jesus, the drying of tears and great joy, it's all left a mark on me. May the Lord in His own way grant some of this insight to you now, in Jesus' name.

We walked back through the gate to the other side where justice, righteousness, and protection travel forth from our faithful God and are carried out in accordance with His will. We headed back toward the sheep gate. Soon, I found myself again standing upon the rock where I first arrived.

Jesus looked like the Lord of glory here—hair the color of light, flaming eyes like pools of fire, great depth of love and justice all rolled into one. As He looked at me, I was no longer afraid but rather instilled with a deep respect. I learned to respect the Lord God Almighty in a manner that has shaped my Christian walk to this very day. Then He spoke to me in words and by thought.

As I have searched the scriptures, I have acquired more truth and understanding, and my heart has been more healed. As my heart became healed, I walked in more freedom and joy. In the process, we learn what faith in God really means—trusting in Him, the faithful God who will see us through. I came away from all this with great respect for the sovereignty of God who helps us become more interwoven with Him throughout our life. But what I learned the most is that He is the faithful God who does not leave us orphans in this world and has prepared a place for us in the world to come.

Standing before Him upon that rock, I did not want to leave. I realized plainly that I needed and wanted Him. When

I stumble, His great grace, His rebuke, and all of life's lessons change the direction of my life. He has my back.

Jesus faced me and I Him. He quietly blew on me, and I departed, gently floating through the peaceful void with its glorious music and choir. I floated back into my bedroom, greeted by the early morning sun shining brightly upon me.

All this happened by His great grace. I was allowed to see a small part of heaven to relieve me from the trauma of seeing hell. I was not asleep. I arose more refreshed than ever. My dog was extremely happy. So I got ready for work by putting my dog outside in the fenced area where a kind neighbor would attend to her needs during the day. I felt better than I ever had before. I recall being so utterly happy and refreshed that day, yet totally without sleep.

Back then I worked as a building and grounds worker at a local department store. My boss looked at me and said, "Bryan, you are glowing, *who were you with last night?*"

I replied simply, "No one," and then excused myself to the restroom to look. Was I glowing? To my eyes, no, I wasn't. Yet customers and kids in the store commented that "this guy is glowing." I recall one small child came to me and said, "Mister, did you see Jesus?" I said yes, and the kid's mother called the child away while looking at me, telling her friend in a low tone, "He's glowing."

I know for a fact that I was not glowing like Moses because people could look at me. I may have simply had a glow of great joy, peace, happiness, compassion, and contentment that lights up a person's countenance, or maybe I was a wee bit brighter than this? I still had to turn on the lights at night, so I was not glowing like a lightbulb. Best I can figure out is that it was an inner glow that came out of me. It lasted three days. During those three days, amazing things happened. After getting home from church or work, I walked with my dog out to the prairie toward a small, tree-lined lake, to a place filled with migrating yellow birds. One sat on the fence chirping. I could have touched it. It felt no fear of me and neither did the thousands of yellow birds that surrounded me and my dog. We were as close as can be without stepping on any. My dog would not chase them away, as is the nature of dogs. I simply wondered at their friendliness. At the time, I never caught on to what was happening.

One time as I sat by the river so my dog could swim, all these animals and birds gathered around me. Ducks in the river quacked on by. A red fox came to drink, looked at me and my dog without worry, and scampered off. My dog was the most well-behaved. She never chased any of these animals away. After three days of this, the animals never did this again. My dog resumed chasing them away as is the norm for dogs. The outward glow had gone away, but to this day it remains deep within me. Great peace. Peace with God. I know Him who is able, amen!

I know this is hard to believe, but it happened. Many bystanders who saw me would say in hushed tones and stares, "Look—he is glowing." It's impossible for me to doubt this happened. You can doubt, and that is okay with me.

* * *

The radio crackled; the weather report ended. Night Ryder was finishing the local monologue and events.

After that, Tina asked, "What did you come away with most after seeing heaven—the thing that struck you most?"

"Well," I replied, "there is so much..."

* * *

What heaven showed me, simply, is that Jesus has me in His hands. He is faithful and true. Jesus Christ is our Advocate. We do not have it easy in life. The devil still comes to rob, kill, and destroy. We stumble and fail at times. Yet God is faithful. He declared us upright, blameless, righteous, and holy in His sight due to the work of Christ on the cross alone.

> *He who calls you is faithful, who also will do it* (1 Thessalonians 5:24 NJKV).

He is the faithful God. He who calls is faithful to perform His word. Either his gifts, callings, and promises are irrevocable or they are not. If not, then He is unable to perform the word spoken and is no longer the faithful God.

Well-meaning Christians lose sight of Him by trusting in their own efforts and works due to a secret need for approval and validation. I did the same after becoming born again. Because I saw hell, I worked very hard to keep myself saved. I never wanted to go back. Seeing heaven revealed to me that I am secure in His hands because I am being changed by His intercession over me as Hebrews 7:25 proclaims. He carries out His word. I trust Him. How about you?

If I stray, He loves me enough to chasten me back to His ways. By that, I learn He really loves and cares for me. He will never let those who are truly His own go. Those who belong to Him learn all their mortal lives to depart from iniquity. Those who do not belong to Him sin, but grace abounds for them. Sadly, in many segments of Christendom, people forget that God's grace teaches us how to live responsibly before Him and toward one another.

God's grace is not a greasy slide into heaven. Heaven is a journey uphill with the One who is faithful. He has you, intercedes over you, and guides you away from satan's Bar and Grill, not to it. So I ask you to trust Him, Jesus Christ.

Our Lord and Savior boldly proclaimed that no one can snatch you and me out of His hand (see John 10:27-30)! If you try to jump ship, He catches you before you hit the ground (see Isaiah 55:6-13). He is the true good shepherd who will leave the flock in good care while He goes after one straying sheep. He will bear the lost sheep on His shoulders and carry it safely back home. So I ask, do you think you are wiser and stronger than God? God pursues you and beckons you to come to Him. I am thankful that the Lord Almighty is a faithful God who chastises us. He draws us back after we taste the bitterness of the world. So the question becomes, can we lose our salvation—is that possible?

Yes, there are those who think one can by simply walking away from the faith. I respect their point of view as they are brothers and sisters in Christ. We are all on the same team. I ask—those who walk away, were they ever really saved to begin with? Receiving the word of God superficially is different from receiving the word deeply, penitently, within a grateful heart (see James 1:21).

The parable of sower in Luke 8 is all about how people receive the word. Receiving the word along the wayside is not the same as receiving it deeply within a willing, grateful, plowed heart. In this parable, the seed sown is called the word of God, the full gospel of Christ that began atop Calvary's hill: "Father, forgive them for they know not what they do!"

Hebrews 4:12-14 says that God's word reveals the thoughts and intents of the human heart. It is doing just that in the parable of the sower. The word of God exposes the nature of the human heart. Then mankind is broken by the word of God just as Jeremiah 23:29 proclaims.

"Is not My word like a fire?" says the Lord, *"And like a hammer that breaks the rock in pieces?"* (Jeremiah 23:29 NKJV)

The wayside is the shallow soil of the world (see Luke 8:12). There, the seed simply lies on the surface, becoming easy for the devil to remove. The word of God doesn't even have a chance to take root.

Next, the stony ground is filled with rocks (see Luke 8:13). Any cracks are filled in with very shallow soil. In some places, a thin layer of soil camouflages the large stones underneath. Some folks live in a thin layer of soil like this. They endure for a bit, but when temptations come, their hard hearts prevent God's word from going deeper and taking root. The faith of these people is shallow so that they fall back into the trappings of the old life.

No matter what Christian veneer you use, the word exposes what captures your heart. Isaiah 1:18-20 is true. The word of God reveals the thoughts and intents of the heart. What we love the most is revealed.

This is how the word of God works. The Bible teaches this plainly in Hebrews 4:12. His word accomplishes what it is intended for. Then there are those whose heart is covered by brambles, thorns, and bushes (see Luke 8:14), choking the word so it never bears any mature fruit. Such soil is depleted of nutrients and the weeds shade the plants from the sun. Here the word reveals what people love the most—the cares of a culture that seeks only self-gratification and riches. Good seed does not do well in a shallow heart whose true intent is to stay in the world's system. So were those wayside, rocky soil, bramble-loving folks ever really saved? Let's find out.

For starters, those who let the word of God be trampled on by the ways of the world conform to the world's standards. It is all about social justice, paying reparations, inviting what God hates into the church for fear of offending anyone. Who do they love the most? God and others, or themselves? Are they saved?

Then there are those who like to camouflage their stony hearts with a thin layer of soil that looks okay. These people emphasize that Jesus came only to bless us. When trials, temptations, and persecutions come that test their roots, they revert back to their old selfish ways. Were these folks ever really saved?

Lastly, the third group can't receive the seed for briars and brambles deplete the nutrients of the soil and stop the sun from producing any real growth. In this instance, people treat God as though He is a genie who appears only to serve them. Are such people really saved?

> *Nevertheless the solid foundation of God stands, having this seal: "The Lord knows those who are His," and, "Let everyone who names the name of Christ depart from iniquity"* (2 Timothy 2:19 NKJV).

But there are those who break up the fallow ground of the heart, producing good, soft soil, and the word takes root (see Luke 8:15; John 16:7-11). A new man or woman is formed by the new birth and bears the fruit of a changed life and is governed by the Holy Spirit.

The word of God uncovers the condition of the heart, preparing it for the plow so that the grace of God grows (see Titus 2:11-15). A plowed heart willingly receives living water. Those are truly saved. Despite their faults, they learn to depart from iniquity and live a repentant life.

If not, such are those whom Jesus mentions in Matthew 7:21-23 and Matthew 25:11-12, "Depart, I never knew you." I add for emphasis, "…because you play games with My grace and love to justify living profanely. My word proves who really owns your heart—depart!"

Receiving the word of God superficially is a far cry from receiving the word deeply within a grateful heart. There are only those who are truly saved and those who are not. Those who are not are those who walk away, never to return, but they were not His from the beginning.

God is faithful and will never let those who truly come to Him leave or forsake Him. By the cross Jesus showed He is faithful and true: "Today you will be with Me in paradise" (see Luke 23:39-43).

Yes, sometimes we flounder in our faith, but the good shepherd picks us up and carries us. Are you floundering? Do you need a lift? We struggle with sin and sometimes fail, but God will get us through (see 1 John 1). We have a Mediator now, an Advocate, Jesus Christ, to help us no matter the battle. We learn grace and love Him even more because He holds us fast in His hands, changing our ways out of the persecutor's darkness into His marvelous light. And we know, because His Word tells us:

God is light and in Him is no darkness at all [not one speck of darkness] (1 John 1:5 NKJV).

The Light of heaven beckons to you and me. Let us bring forth His light on earth as it is in heaven.

ADDENDA

CLOSING THOUGHTS

I did not write this to make myself out as someone great. I am not. Nor did I share these things to glory myself. I can care less about fame, acclaim, renown. My aim is to lift Jesus up so that you look to Him and not me.

This book was difficult to write. The reason why is simply that my experience was more personal. Its purpose was to help me overcome seeing hell during the summer of 1980.

I should not be here writing any of this. It is a miracle by God's grace that I even survived. Therefore, when I say I owe Him my life, I mean it. So, I ask shouldn't the gospel have the same effect on people today?

About the Characters Mentioned in the Book

In this book I use the literary style of creative nonfiction. The names of people mentioned are formed from composites of several people. No real names were used. The conversations between people were added to aid the flow of the story.

The event with Betty happened. The conversations with her were added according to my best recollection. Betty is not her real name.

The radio interview is based on multitudes of the interviews I have done. The station's call sign is not real. Thus, the radio personalities are composites of many radio hosts and podcasters all over the country.

Pastor Loos is based on all the great pastors who helped mentor me. The church and what happened is based on events seen in several churches.

I tried to capture some the flakiness I witnessed in churches in the first few chapters of this book to reveal how Jesus works through all this, refining His people in ways which removes our dross.

I amplified these events into one night to make an important point hit home: God uses us despite our flaws.

I did take inebriated people to church, and they sometimes did some wild things that embarrassed me. The events with Tom are a composite of several such people rolled into one to protect their identity. These events did happen.

The pastors I knew back then took it all in stride, showing great patience, kindness, and care. We always need more men of God like this.

The events I described leading to my departure to heaven happened. The light and booming voice happened. My three responses are real. Jesus has amazing grace and patience with us all. I rejoice in this! Amen!

Some folks asked me about my writing style due to some of the poetic flow I use. I am dyslexic. I had poor reading skills and comprehension growing up. My spelling was atrocious, and I failed fourth grade because of it. My fifth-grade teacher saw something in a story I wrote about two civil war soldiers accidently shooting their beloved leader. Although my spelling was terrible, I received a good grade for content.

My teacher helped improve my reading comprehension by having me select what I like to read, which is history. She worked on my spelling. It improved. I developed a knack for writing poetry and often would add its metered prose within my writing projects.

I owe a debt of gratitude to my fifth-grade teacher, who was also my sixth-grade teacher. She inspired me to write and love reading. I am grateful to her; she saw something in me I never knew I had. That is how Jesus sees you and me. He uses folks in our lives to get that through to us.

With that, hats off to all great teachers who take the time and effort to help students like me. We need more teachers like this. Maybe you'll be one?

So if you have some disability like this or another, never think you are not valued by God or that He cannot use you. Maybe, just maybe, this happened in your life so you can help others in ways no one else can.

A Message from Heaven Needed for This Hour

Lastly, there is a message from heaven I would like to end with. The modern church has become distracted. Thus evil, along with its depravity, runs amuck. We will soon reach a point without remedy just as 2 Chronicles 36:16 describes.

Much of the modern church seeks signs and wonders but not the Giver. Occult works have entered in claiming that since there are counterfeits, the counterfeits must look like the real without really knowing what the real looks like to make an honest comparison.

There are those distracted by dogma rather than their first love for Christ. Others are distracted by letting culture rule the church and being like the world. Then there is the distraction where the gospel becomes concerned with formulas, health, gaining wealth, and about you becoming the new "I am."

Second Chronicles 7:14 tells God's people to turn away from their warped, twisted ways and trying to use God's good nature for their own ends. The Lord will burn away such wood, hay, and stubble at an appointed time, but for others, not so.

One thing I learned from heaven is the need for a greater appreciation of who and what God is like. We need a revival of this on earth today before the point of no return is reached.

I hope this book will in some way cause you to get into your Bible and explore what God is like. You'll be amazed how that straightens out the mind and keeps us all on track. It frees us from the distractions that have let the enemy gain dominance over the world. Is there a cure? Yes!

Seeing heaven helped me see God's sovereign hand working in ways in complete accord with His character traits, with no shadow of turning. He is slow to anger, but a time without remedy will one day will be reached (see Revelation 2 and 3).

Much was revealed to me about God's character and nature in heaven, and how people use these for their own ends and glory. I attempted to share some of these with you in this book. For what purpose?

We need to gaze on God, look to Him, study His ways. The more we learn what He says about Himself in the Bible, the less we will abuse His character traits, nature, and word to justify our distractions. We need a revival concerning who God really is so we can see the error of our ways and turn from them.

In some way, I ask that He impart who He is and what He is like into all who read this book. May such a revival come, as it is written:

Look to Me, and be saved, all you ends of the earth! For I am God, and there is no other (Isaiah 45:22 NKJV).

God bless you all, in Jesus' name!

ABOUT B.W. MELVIN

B.W. Melvin is a graduate of Colorado State University where he received his degree in Social Work with emphasis in the field of criminal Justice. Bryan's career path includes counseling, criminal justice, case management, and managing treatment teams for violent criminal offenders.

He is an author, evangelist, and public speaker appearing both on TV and radio and is currently involved in Christian evangelistic work. Bryan's first book, *A Land Unknown: Hell's Dominion*, is based on his personal after-death experience changing the lives of many for Christ.

Made in the USA
Las Vegas, NV
01 August 2024

93260233R00125